Eyewitness
HUMAN BODY

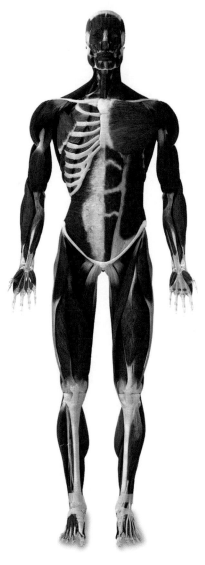

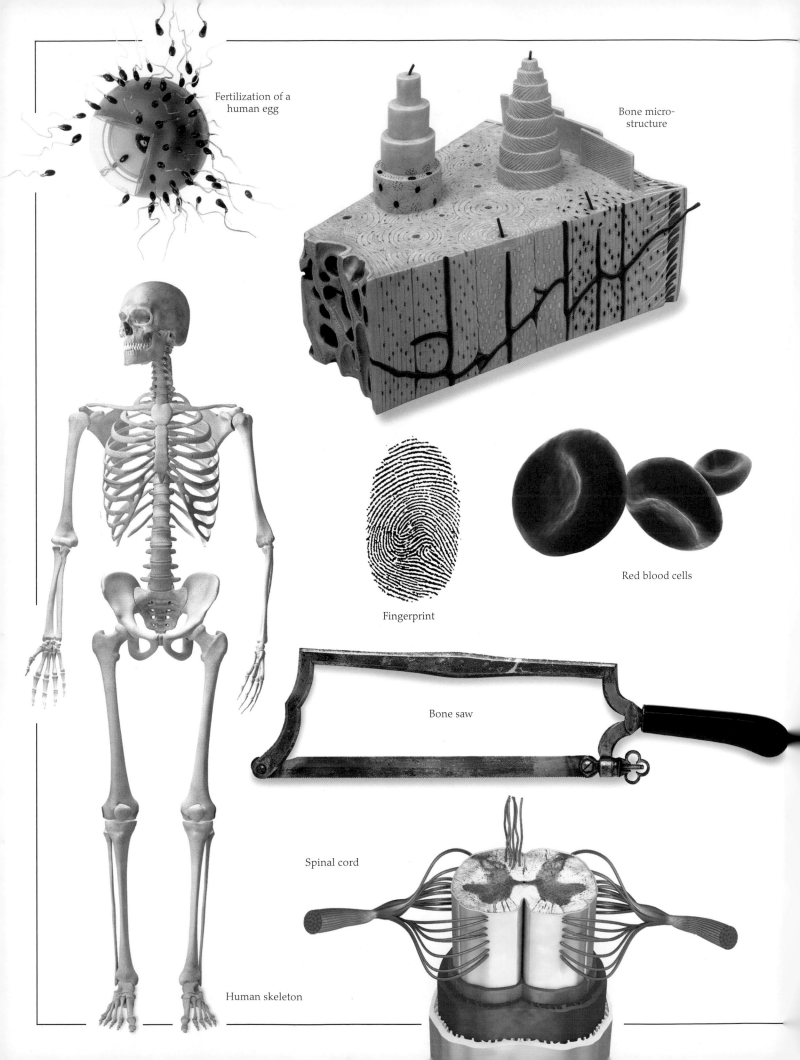

Fertilization of a human egg

Bone micro-structure

Fingerprint

Red blood cells

Bone saw

Spinal cord

Human skeleton

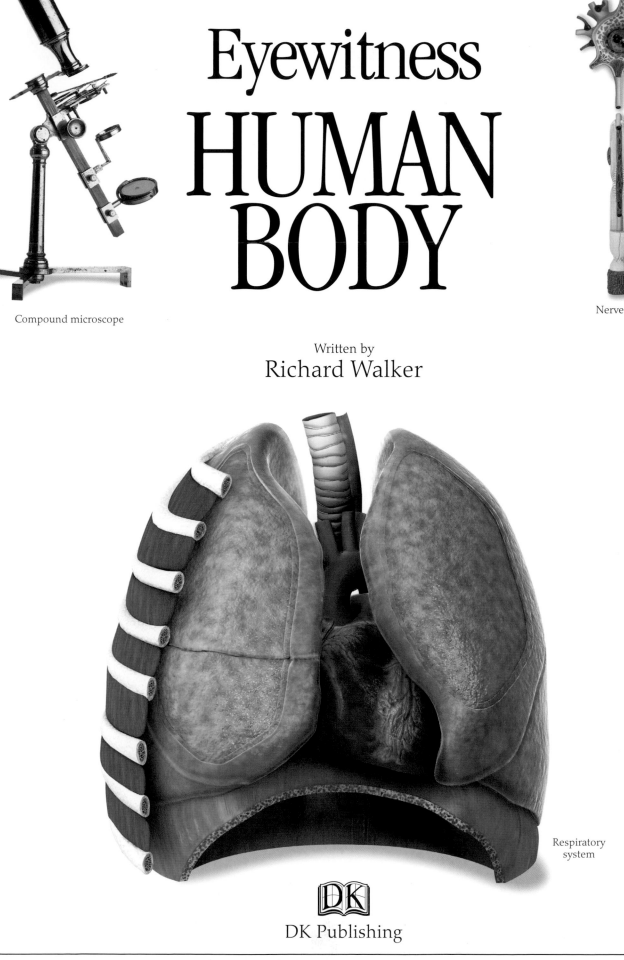

Compound microscope

Eyewitness
HUMAN
BODY

Nerve cell

Written by
Richard Walker

Respiratory
system

DK Publishing

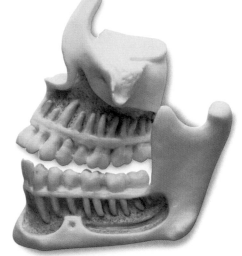

Chromosome

19th-century clamping forceps

Cross-section of the skin

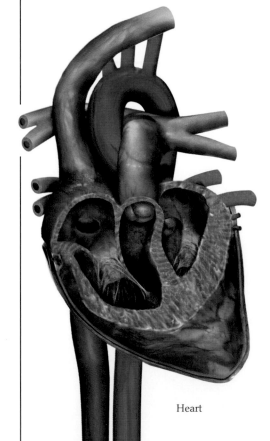

Adult teeth

DK

LONDON, NEW YORK, MUNICH,
MELBOURNE, AND DELHI

Editor Lisa Stock
Project editor Jane Yorke
Art editor David Ball
Senior editor Rob Houston
Senior art editor Alison Gardner
Managing editor Camilla Hallinan
Managing art editor Owen Peyton Jones
Art director Martin Wilson
Category publisher Andrew Macintyre
Picture researcher Louise Thomas
Production editor Hitesh Patel
Senior production controller Pip Tinsley
Jacket designer Andy Smith

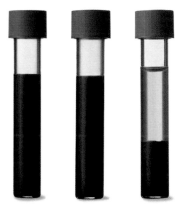

Oxygen-rich   Oxygen-poor   Settled
blood   blood   blood

First published in the United States in 2009 by
DK Publishing, 375 Hudson Street, New York, New York 10014

Copyright © 2009 Dorling Kindersley Limited

09 10 11 12 13 10 9 8 7 6 5 4 3 2
ED745 – 01/09

Some of the material in this book previously appeared in
Eyewitness Human Body, published in 1993, 2004.

Published in Great Britain by Dorling Kindersley Limited.

A catalog record for this book is available
from the Library of Congress.

ISBN 978-0-7566-4545-8 (HC); 978-0-7566-4533-5 (ALB)

Color reproduction by Colourscan, Singapore.
Printed and bound by Toppan Printing Co. (Shenzen) Ltd., China.

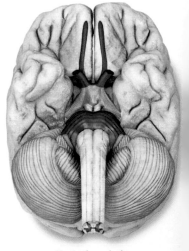

Brain from below

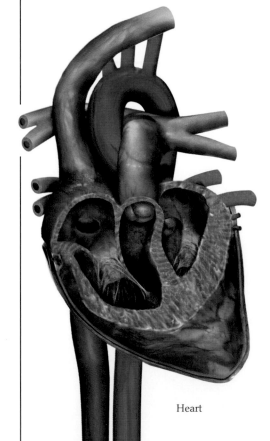

Heart

Discover more at
www.dk.com

Contents

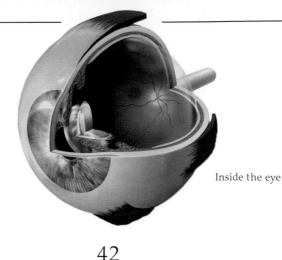

Inside the eye

The human body

HUMAN ORIGINS
The earliest humans evolved from an apelike ancestor millions of years ago. Over time they started to walk upright and developed larger brains. The many different human species included this tool-using *Homo habilis*, from around two million years ago. Modern humans are the sole survivors of a many-branched family tree.

HUMAN BEINGS ARE THE MOST INTELLIGENT creatures on Earth. This intelligence, linked with natural curiosity, gives us a unique opportunity to understand our own bodies. Knowledge gained over centuries tells us that while we may look different from the outside, our bodies are all constructed in the same way. The study of anatomy, which explores body structure, shows that internally we are virtually identical—aside from differences between males and females. The study of physiology, which deals with how the body works, reveals how body systems combine to keep our cells, and us, alive. Human beings are all related. We belong to the species *Homo sapiens*, and are descendants of the first modern humans, who lived in Africa 160,000 years ago and later migrated across the globe.

UNDERSTANDING ANATOMY
The modern study of anatomy dates back to the Renaissance period in the 15th and 16th centuries. For the first time, it became legal to dissect, or cut open, a dead body in order to examine its parts in minute detail. These accurate drawings of the muscular and skeletal systems are the result of such dissections. The images are taken from a groundbreaking book published by Renaissance doctor Andreas Vesalius (p. 10), one of the pioneers of human anatomy.

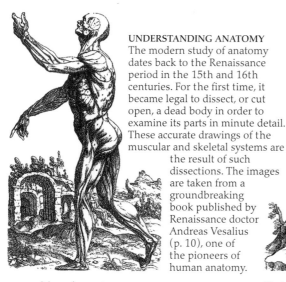

Muscular system

Skeletal system

Eye is a light-detecting sense organ

Vein carries the blood towards the heart

Artery carries the blood away from the heart

Nerve carries electrical signals to and from the brain

Bone supports the upper arm

THE BODY AND THE BUILDING
In 1708, one explanation of human physiology likened the body to the workings of a household. It compared their functions such as bringing in supplies (eating food), distributing essentials (the blood system), creating warmth (body chemical processes), and organizing the household (the brain).

WORKING TOGETHER
Body organs and systems cannot exist in isolation. With its skin and some muscles removed, this body shows how the internal organs and systems work together to keep us alive. Bones, muscles, and cartilage provide support and movement. Nerves carry control signals. The heart and blood vessels deliver food everywhere, along with oxygen taken in through the lungs. As a result of this cooperation, the body maintains a balanced internal environment, with a constant temperature of 98.6°F (37°C). This enables cells to work at their best.

Body construction

It takes around 100 trillion cells to build a human body. There are 200 different types of these microscopic living units, each of which is highly complex. Similar cells join together to make a tissue, two or more tissues form an organ, and linked organs create a system. Body systems interact to form a living human being. To understand how this arrangement works, see the digestive system (right).

Cartilage supports the nose

Teeth cut up food during eating

Neck muscle moves the head

Lung gets oxygen into the body

Heart pumps the blood

Tendon attaches a muscle to bone

Liver cleans the blood

1 SYSTEM
The digestive system is just one of 12 body systems. The others are the skin, skeletal, muscular, nervous, hormonal, circulatory, lymphatic, immune, respiratory, urinary, and reproductive systems. The role of the digestive system is to break down food so it can be used by body cells. Each of its organs, including the stomach and small intestine, play their part in this process.

Small intestine

Digestive system

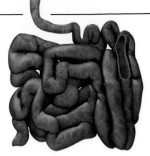

2 ORGAN
The small intestine is a long digestive tube. It completes the breakdown of food into simple substances, which are absorbed into the blood. Muscle tissue in the wall of the small intestine pushes food along it. Other tissues supply blood and nerve signals. Epithelial tissues lining the small intestine control food absorption into the blood.

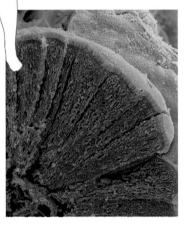

3 TISSUE
The lining of the small intestine has millions of microscopic fingerlike projections called villi. The tissue covering villi is called columnar epithelium (orange). Its outer surface is covered with tiny microvilli (green). Together this tissue provides a vast surface for absorbing food.

4 CELLS
The epithelial cells covering a villus are tightly clumped together. This organization stops food and digestive juices from leaking through to the tissues below, which support these cells. As they suffer great wear and tear, epithelial cells are replaced every few days.

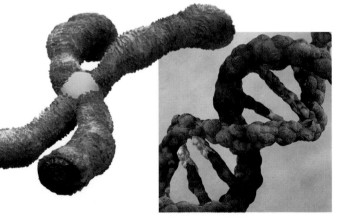

5 CHROMOSOME
Every cell has a control center, called its nucleus, which contains 46 chromosomes. Normally the chromosomes exist as long threads, but they coil up tightly into an X-shape (above), when a cell divides. Chromosomes contain the coded instructions, called genes, that are needed for building the body's cells, tissues, organs, and systems.

6 DNA
Each chromosome consists of a molecule called deoxyribonucleic acid (DNA). DNA has two twisted strands that form a double-helix (double-spiral) shape. The DNA strands are linked by chemicals called bases (blue, green, red, yellow). The sequence of different bases provides a gene's coded instructions for building or controlling the body.

Myths, magic, and medicine

THOUSANDS OF YEARS AGO, EARLY HUMANS made sculptures and cave paintings of figures with recognizable human body shapes. As civilizations developed, people started to think about the world around them and study their own bodies more closely. The ancient Egyptians, for example, mummified millions of bodies, but little of their anatomical knowledge has survived. Until the time of the ancient Greeks, medicine—or the care and treatment of the sick and injured—remained tied up with myths, magic, and superstition, and a belief that gods or demons sent illnesses. The "father of medicine," Greek physician Hippocrates (c. 460–377 BCE) taught that diseases were not sent by the gods, but were medical conditions that could be identified and treated. During the Roman Empire, Galen (129–c. 216 CE) established theories about anatomy and physiology that would last for centuries. As Roman influence declined, medical knowledge spread east to Persia, where the teachings of Hippocrates and Galen were developed by physicians such as Avicenna (980–1037 CE).

PREHISTORIC ART
This Aboriginal rock art is from Kakudu National Park in Australia. It was painted with natural pigments made from plant saps and minerals. X-ray figures showing the internal anatomy of humans and animals have featured in Aboriginal art for 4,000 years.

HOLES IN THE HEAD
This 4,000-year-old skull from Jericho, in present-day Israel, shows the results of trepanning, or drilling holes in the skull. This was probably carried out to expose the brain and release evil spirits. The holes show partial healing, which indicates that people could survive this age-old procedure. Modern surgery uses a similar technique, called craniotomy, to cut an opening in the skull and release pressure in the brain caused by bleeding.

SURGICAL SACRIFICE
Several ancient cultures sacrificed animals and humans to please their gods and spirits. In the 14th and 15th centuries, the Aztecs dominated present-day Mexico. They believed their Sun-and-war god Huitzilopochtli would make the Sun rise and bring them success in battle, if offered daily blood, limbs, and hearts torn from living human sacrifices. From these grisly rituals, the Aztecs learned about the inner organs of the body.

EGYPTIAN PRESERVATION
Some 5,000 years ago, the Egyptians believed that a dead body remained home to its owner's soul in the afterlife, but only if preserved as a lifelike mummy. First, body organs were removed and stored in jars. Then natron, a type of salt, was used to dry out the body to embalm it and stop it from rotting. Finally, the body was perfumed with oils, wrapped in cloth, and placed in a tomb.

Internal organs, removed from an opening in the side, were preserved separately in special jars

Brain, regarded as useless, was hooked out through the nostrils and discarded

Heart, seen as the center of being, was left inside the chest

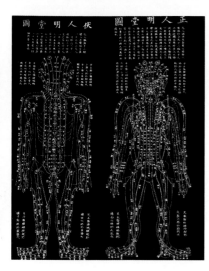

CHINESE CHANNELS

Written in China over 2,300 years ago, *The Yellow Emperor's Classic of Internal Medicine* describes some parts of the body, but contains little detailed knowledge of anatomy. It explains acupuncture treatments, which focus on the flow of unseen chi, or vital energy, along 12 body channels known as meridians. Needles are inserted into the skin along these meridians. This restores energy flow and good health by rebalancing the body forces known as Yin (cool and female) and Yang (hot and male).

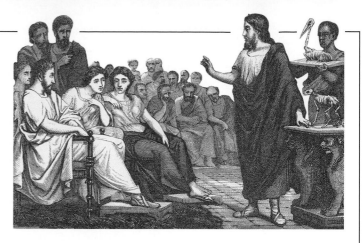

CLAUDIUS GALEN

Born in ancient Greece, physician Claudius Galen spent much of his life in Rome, where he became a towering figure in the study of anatomy, physiology, and medicine. As a young physician Galen treated gladiators, describing their wounds as "windows into the body." At this time, human dissection (pp. 10–11) was forbidden by law, so Galen studied the anatomy of animals, believing his observations would apply to the human body. This explains why, despite his many discoveries, Galen made some serious errors. His flawed ideas were accepted without question for nearly 1,500 years.

Galen remained a great influence in Europe and the Islamic world for many centuries

Hippocrates believed that physicians should act in their patients' best interests

MEDIEVAL TREATMENTS

Bloodletting, using a knife or a bloodsucking worm called a leech, was a traditional, if brutal, remedy for all kinds of ills in medieval times. Few physicians tried to see if the treatment was of any benefit to the patient. Scientific assessments, such as keeping medical records and checking up on the progress of patients, were not developed until the 17th century.

SAVING KNOWLEDGE

This illustration is taken from the 1610 translation of the *Canon Of Medicine*. Persian physician Avicenna wrote this medical encyclopedia in c. 1025. He was the first to conduct experimental medicine on the human body. He tested new drugs and studied their effectiveness on patients. Avicenna built on the knowledge of Galen and Hippocrates, whose medical works survived only because they were taken to Persia, translated, and spread through the Islamic world. Their ideas were reintroduced to Europe after Islam spread to Spain in 711 CE.

Embalming process dried out the muscles, which shrank and exposed the bones

Avicenna, the Persian anatomist, built on the teachings of the Romans and Greeks

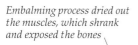

Skin became dark and leathery through embalming and age

Toenails, being made of dead cells, remained intact

Study and dissection

It is not surprising that the teachings of physician Claudius Galen (pp. 8–9) included errors, since he based them on studies of the insides of animals and the wounds of Roman gladiators. Tradition and religion forbade any criticism of Galen's work during the Middle Ages between the 5th and 15th centuries. The same oppressive attitude prevented the practice of dissection, the precise cutting open of a body to study its internal structure. With the dawn of the Renaissance, however, that ban was relaxed. This rebirth of the arts, architecture, and science spread across Europe between the 14th and 17th centuries. In Italy, Andreas Vesalius (1514–64) performed careful, accurate dissections and drew his own conclusions, based on his observations, rather than blindly repeating the centuries-old accepted views. By questioning and correcting Galen's teachings, Vesalius revolutionized the science of anatomy and initiated a new era in medicine.

RESPECT FOR DEATH
For many people in the Middle Ages, life was less important than what came afterward—death, and ascent into heaven. The body was the soul's temporary home. Earthly matters, such as what was inside the body, were unimportant. Dissection was forbidden, and this anatomist may well have been punished.

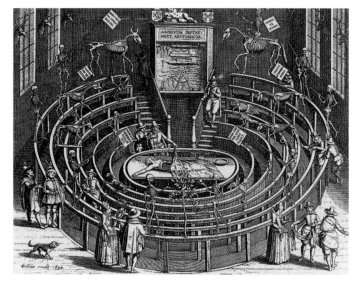

ANATOMICAL THEATER
Mondino dei Liuzzi (c. 1270–1326), a professor at Bologna, Italy, is known as the Restorer of Anatomy. He introduced the dissection of human corpses, but still relied heavily on Galen's theories. His 1316 manual, *Anatomy*, remained popular until Vesalius's time. By the late 16th century, the quest for knowledge about the body caught the public's imagination, and anatomical theaters were built at numerous universities. This 1610 engraving shows the anatomical theater at Leiden, in the Netherlands. Spectators in the gallery looked down as the anatomy professor or his assistant carried out a dissection.

Strong, thick metal frame

End screw to remove blade

BREAK WITH TRADITION
During the 16th century, Padua was at the forefront of Italian anatomy and medicine. In 1536, Andreas Vesalius arrived. His exceptional skills were soon evident, and the following year he became professor of anatomy. After translating early medical texts, Vesalius became dissatisfied with the teachings from ancient times. He preferred to believe what he saw in front of him, and set about writing his own book. When he had completed it, Vesalius became physician to Spanish royalty.

FIRST SCIENTIFIC ANATOMY BOOK
Four intense years of dissection produced Vesalius's *On the Structure of the Human Body*, published in 1543. The stunning lifelike-in-death illustrations and descriptive text caused sensation and outrage, since they went against traditional teachings.

SUBJECTS FOR STUDY

Hanged criminals were a steady source of specimens for dissection. In *The Anatomy Lesson of Dr. Nicholaes Tulp* (1632), a famous painting by the Dutch artist Rembrandt, the dissection subject was robber Aris Kindt. The painting shows Dr. Tulp demonstrating how dissected forearm flexor muscles bend the fingers. Anatomy lessons were training for physicians and surgeons, and were open to anyone from the public who was interested.

WOMEN AND ANATOMY

Until the 19th century, human structure and function were studied almost exclusively by men. Women took on only very minor medical roles, except as midwifes. This profession has always been almost exclusively female. These Swedish women learning anatomy, in a photograph from about 1880, are probably training for midwifery.

Double-ended small probe

Fine end

Bulbous end

Hooked point

Hooked needle

Wooden handle

Skull removed to expose brain

Blade can be sharpened for use

Scalpel

Fine forceps (tweezers)

Needlelike tips

Ridged, splayed tips for gripping

Clamping forceps

Handles have a scissor design

Muscle layer peeled back

TOOLS OF THE TRADE

These 19th-century surgical instruments evolved from the knives, scissors, saws, and probes that were used by Renaissance anatomists such as Vesalius. Today's surgeons use a similar but broader range of instruments, making use of modern technology, such as power saws and laser scalpels. Each instrument has its own role, from cutting through tough bones to probing tiny nerves and blood vessels.

WAX MODEL

Crafted from wax, this extraordinary anatomical model shows the dissected head and neck of a man, including muscles, nerves, blood vessels, and the brain. In the 18th and 19th centuries, accurately colored, three-dimensional wax models like this one provided excellent teaching aids for trainee doctors.

Instruments illustrated in the second edition of Vesalius's book, 1555

Serrated saw blade

Large bone saw

Tensioning screw to tighten blade

Wooden handle shaped to fit palm of hand

The microscopic body

At the beginning of the 1600s, scientific instrument makers in the Netherlands invented a magnifying device called the microscope. For the first time, scientists used high-quality glass lenses to view objects, illuminated by light, which previously had been far too small to see with the naked eye. Among these pioneering microscopists were Antoni van Leeuwenhoek and Marcello Malpighi. Using their own versions of the microscope, they showed that living things are made up of much smaller units. In 1665, a founding member of England's Royal Society (an organization of top scientists that still exists today) devised a name for those units—"cells." Robert Hooke (1635–1703) had seen microscopic, boxlike compartments in plant tissue that he likened to the cells, or rooms, of monks in a monastery. The term has been used ever since. In the 20th century, a new type of microscope was invented that used electrons instead of light. Today the electron microscope allows scientists to discover much more about the structure and workings of cells.

PIONEER HISTOLOGIST
Italian scientist Marcello Malpighi (1628–94) was the founder of microscopic anatomy and a pioneer of histology, the study of tissues. Malpighi was the first to identify capillaries, the tiny blood vessels that connect arteries to veins. He also described the filtering units inside the kidneys. In 1668, Malpighi became the first Italian to be elected a fellow of the Royal Society.

Lens held between two plates

WIDE-RANGING OBSERVER
Antoni van Leeuwenhoek (1632–1723) was a Dutch cloth merchant who developed a hobby as a self-taught scientist and microscopist. With his homemade microscopes he was the first to observe, among many other things, blood cells and sperm. In 1683 he spotted, in scrapings from his own teeth, the first bacteria seen by the human eye. The Royal Society published many of his descriptions, and he was eventually elected a fellow of the Society.

Pin to hold the specimen in place

Screw to bring the specimen into focus

Handle to hold the lens close to the eye

Eyepiece lens magnifies the image produced by the objective lens

Powerful objective lens collects light from the specimen to create an image

Lens tube

Stage holds the specimen

Specimen illuminated with light from below

Lens focuses light rays from the mirror

Screw adjusts the stage height for focusing

Mirror reflects light from a lamp or window

Tripod base

HOMEMADE LENSES
Most microscopes in van Leeuwenhoek's day had two lenses, as shown on the right. His version, shown life-size above, had one tiny lens, which he made himself using a secret technique. His lenses produced a view that was amazingly sharp and clear. He was able to observe cells, tissues, and tiny organisms magnified up to 275 times. Van Leeuwenhoek made about 400 microscopes in all, and helped to establish microscopy as a branch of science.

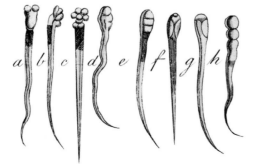
a b c d e f g h i

MICROSCOPIC DRAWINGS
Today, photography is commonly used to produce a permanent record of what is viewed under the microscope. Early microscopists such as Malpighi, van Leeuwenhoek, and Hooke used drawings and modern writing to record what they had seen. This drawing by van Leeuwenhoek records his observation, for the first time, of sperm cells, one of his most important discoveries.

COMPOUND MICROSCOPE
Van Leeuwenhoek's microscopes are called "simple" because they had only one lens. But most light microscopes—ones that use light for illuminating the specimen—are compound, using two or more lenses. This 19th-century model has all the basic features found on a modern compound microscope. Its specimen stage moves up and down to focus, whereas in newer models the lens tube moves. The specimen is sliced thinly enough for light to be shone through it and up through the lenses to the eye.

INSIDE A CELL

This cutaway model of a typical human cell shows the parts of a cell that can be seen using an electron microscope. A thin cell membrane surrounds the cell. The jellylike cytoplasm contains structures, called organelles (small organs), and each has its own supporting role. The nucleus, the largest structure within the cell, contains the instructions needed to run the cell. Every second, thousands of chemical reactions occur inside the cytoplasm, organelles, and nucleus. Together they make up the cell's metabolism, the engine that keeps it alive. Although cells vary greatly in size, shape, and function, they all share the same basic structure and metabolism.

Electron gun

Organelles called endoplasmic reticulum transport proteins for cell metabolism

ELECTRON MICROSCOPE

An electron microscope uses minute parts of atoms called electrons to magnify thousands or millions of times. This reveals the detail of objects too small to be seen with a light microscope. The microscope consists of a column with an electron gun at the top and a specimen stage toward the base. The gun fires an electron beam, focused by magnets, toward a specimen. Electrons that pass through or bounce off the specimen are detected and create an image on a monitor.

Nucleus is the cell's control center

Organelles called mitochondria provide energy for metabolism

Microtubule supports and shapes the cell

Cytoplasm in which the organelles float and move

Organelle called the Golgi body processes proteins for use inside or outside the cell

Cell membrane controls movement of substances in and out of the cell

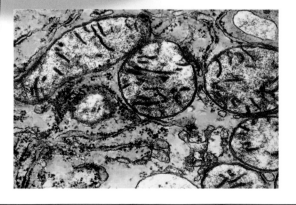

CELL SLICE

A transmission electron microscope projects an electron beam through a slice of body tissue onto a monitor. The resulting image is photographed to produce a transmission electron micrograph (TEM). This TEM has been coloured to show a slice of liver cell magnified 11,300 times to reveal its mitochondria (white), and endoplasmic reticulum (blue).

SURFACE VIEW

In a scanning electron microscope, an electron beam scans the surface of a whole specimen. Electrons bouncing off the specimen are focused to produce a black-and-white, three-dimensional image. A scanning electron micrograph (SEM) is a photograph of that image. This SEM, to which color has been added, shows the surface of rounded fat cells, magnified 530 times.

Looking inside the body

UNTIL THE 19TH CENTURY, THE ONLY WAY of looking inside the body was to cut it open or to inspect the wounds of injured soldiers. The invention of the ophthalmoscope in 1851, a forerunner of instruments used today, allowed doctors to view the inside of a patient's eye for the first time. In 1895, German physicist Wilhelm Roentgen (1845–1923) discovered X-rays and showed that they could produce images of bones without cutting open the body. In addition to X-rays, today's doctors and scientists have access to a wide range of body imaging techniques invented in the past 40 years. These techniques allow them to view tissues and search for signs of disease, and to find out how the body works.

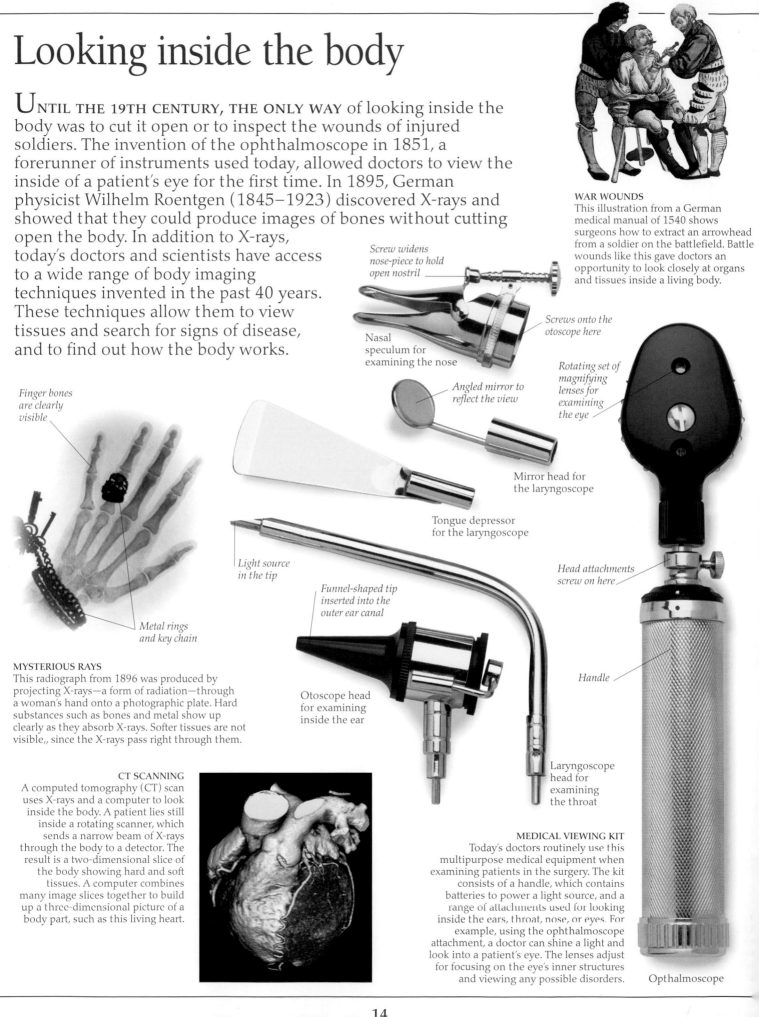

WAR WOUNDS
This illustration from a German medical manual of 1540 shows surgeons how to extract an arrowhead from a soldier on the battlefield. Battle wounds like this gave doctors an opportunity to look closely at organs and tissues inside a living body.

Screw widens nose-piece to hold open nostril

Screws onto the otoscope here

Nasal speculum for examining the nose

Angled mirror to reflect the view

Rotating set of magnifying lenses for examining the eye

Finger bones are clearly visible

Mirror head for the laryngoscope

Tongue depressor for the laryngoscope

Light source in the tip

Funnel-shaped tip inserted into the outer ear canal

Head attachments screw on here

Metal rings and key chain

MYSTERIOUS RAYS
This radiograph from 1896 was produced by projecting X-rays—a form of radiation—through a woman's hand onto a photographic plate. Hard substances such as bones and metal show up clearly as they absorb X-rays. Softer tissues are not visible,, since the X-rays pass right through them.

Otoscope head for examining inside the ear

Handle

Laryngoscope head for examining the throat

CT SCANNING
A computed tomography (CT) scan uses X-rays and a computer to look inside the body. A patient lies still inside a rotating scanner, which sends a narrow beam of X-rays through the body to a detector. The result is a two-dimensional slice of the body showing hard and soft tissues. A computer combines many image slices together to build up a three-dimensional picture of a body part, such as this living heart.

MEDICAL VIEWING KIT
Today's doctors routinely use this multipurpose medical equipment when examining patients in the surgery. The kit consists of a handle, which contains batteries to power a light source, and a range of attachments used for looking inside the ears, throat, nose, or eyes. For example, using the ophthalmoscope attachment, a doctor can shine a light and look into a patient's eye. The lenses adjust for focusing on the eye's inner structures and viewing any possible disorders.

Opthalmoscope

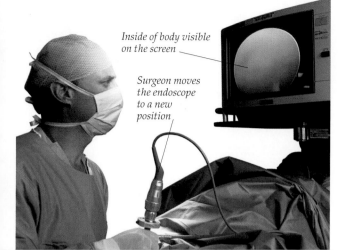

Inside of body visible on the screen

Surgeon moves the endoscope to a new position

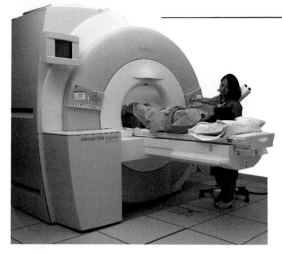

ENDOSCOPE
Surgeons use a thin, tubelike instrument called an endoscope to examine tissues and to look inside joints. An endoscope can be inserted through a natural body opening, such as the mouth, or through a small incision in the skin, as shown here. Long, optical fibers inside the endoscope carry bright light to illuminate the inside of the body and send back images, which are viewed on a monitor.

MAGNETS AND RADIO WAVES
A magnetic resonance imaging (MRI) scanner uses magnets and radio waves to produce images of tissues and organs. Inside the scanner, a patient is exposed to a powerful magnetic field that lines up the hydrogen atoms inside their body. Bursts of radio waves then knock the atoms back to their normal position. When the magnetic field lines the atoms up again they send out tiny radio signals. Different tissues send out differing signals that are detected and turned into images by a computer.

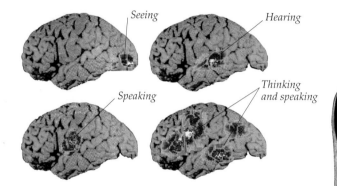

Seeing

Hearing

Speaking

Thinking and speaking

WORKING TISSUES
Positron emission tomography (PET) scans reveal how active specific body tissues are. First, a special form of glucose (sugar) is injected into the bloodstream to provide food energy for hard-working tissues. As the tissues consume the glucose, particles are released that can be detected to form an image. These scans show the areas of brain activity (red/yellow) when a person is seeing, hearing, speaking, and thinking. Results such as these have been used to map the brain (p. 29).

Brain inside the skull

Left lung inside the chest

FULL BODY SCAN
This MRI scan shows a vertical cross-section through a man's body. This is produced by combining many individual scans made along the length of the body. The original black-and-white image has been color enhanced to highlight different tissues and organs. In the head, for example, the brain is colored green; in the chest the lungs are blue; and the larger bones of the skeleton are orange.

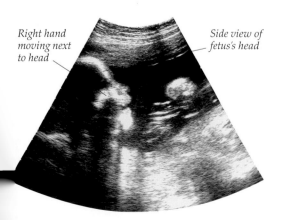

Right hand moving next to head

Side view of fetus's head

Urinary bladder in the lower abdomen

Femur (thigh bone) extends from the hip to the knee

Fleshy calf muscle in the lower leg

FROM SOUND TO IMAGE
Ultrasound scanning is a completely safe way of viewing moving images such as this fetus inside its mother's womb. High-pitched, inaudible sound waves are beamed into the body and are reflected back by tissues. These echoes are then converted into images by a computer.

VIDEO PILL
This capsule endoscope or video pill can be used to identify damage or disease inside the digestive system. It contains a tiny camera, light source, and a transmitter. After being swallowed, the video pill travels along the digestive system, taking pictures on its journey. These images are transmitted to an outside receiver so that a doctor can diagnose any problems.

The body's framework

SYMBOL OF DEATH
Skeletons are enduring symbols of danger, disease, death, and destruction—as seen in this 15th-century *Dance of Death* drawing. In medieval times, the skeletons of gallows victims were left swaying in the breeze on the hangman's noose, as a warning to others.

ONCE A HUMAN BODY HAS REACHED THE END of its life, its softer parts rot away to leave behind a hard, inner framework of 206 bones. This flexible, bony structure is called the skeleton and, in a living person, it serves to support and shape the body. The skeleton surrounds and protects organs such as the brain and heart, and stops them from being jolted or crushed. Bones also provide anchorage for the muscles that move the skeleton and, therefore, the whole body. Bones remain tough and durable long after death and so the anatomists of the past were able to study them in detail. This is why reasonably accurate descriptions of the human skeleton found their way into many early medical textbooks. Today, doctors and scientists use technology, such as the CT scan (p. 14), to examine bones in place inside a living body.

UNDERSTANDING BONES
For centuries, bones were regarded as hard, lifeless supporters of the active, softer tissues around them. Gradually, anatomists saw that bones, though rigid, were very much alive with their own blood vessels and nerves. Here, the renowned medieval surgeon Guy de Chauliac, author of *Great Surgery* (1363), examines a fracture, or broken bone.

Spinal cord is protected by the vertebrae

HUMAN BACKBONE
The backbone, or spine, is a strong, flexible rod that keeps the body upright. It consists of a column of 33 vertebrae. Five of these bones are fused (joined together) in the sacrum and four more bones are fused to form the coccyx (tail of the spine). Each vertebra has a centrum, which bears the body's weight. A pad of cartilage (p. 21), called an intervertebral disk, forms a cushion between one centrum and the next. This arrangement allows limited movement between neighboring vertebrae. However, all of these tiny movements added together along the length of the backbone enable the body to bend forward, backward, side to side, and to twist.

Spinous process

Centrum (body) of the vertebra

Intervertebral disk of cartilage

Centrum

Early 19th-century drawing of a lumbar (lower back) vertebra, seen from above

BODY MECHANICS
A skeleton demonstrates several principles of mechanics. For example, each arm has two sets of long bones that can extend the reach of the hand, or fold back on themselves. Engineers have copied these principles in the design of machines, such as these cranes.

Spinous process (bump) for muscle attachment makes the backbone feel knobbly

Lumbar (lower back) section of the spine

Phalanges (toe bones) of smaller toe

Phalanges of big toe

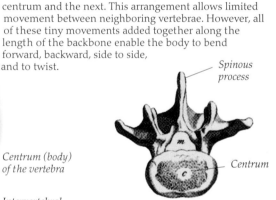

Metatarsals (sole bones)

Tarsals (ankle bones)

Talus connects to the tibia (shin bone) and fibula

Calcaneus (heel bone)

BONES OF THE FOOT
The feet bear the whole weight of the body and each one is made up of 26 bones. There are seven firmly linked tarsals in the ankle (including the talus and calcaneus), five metatarsals in the sole, and three phalanges in each toe, aside from the big toe, which has two.

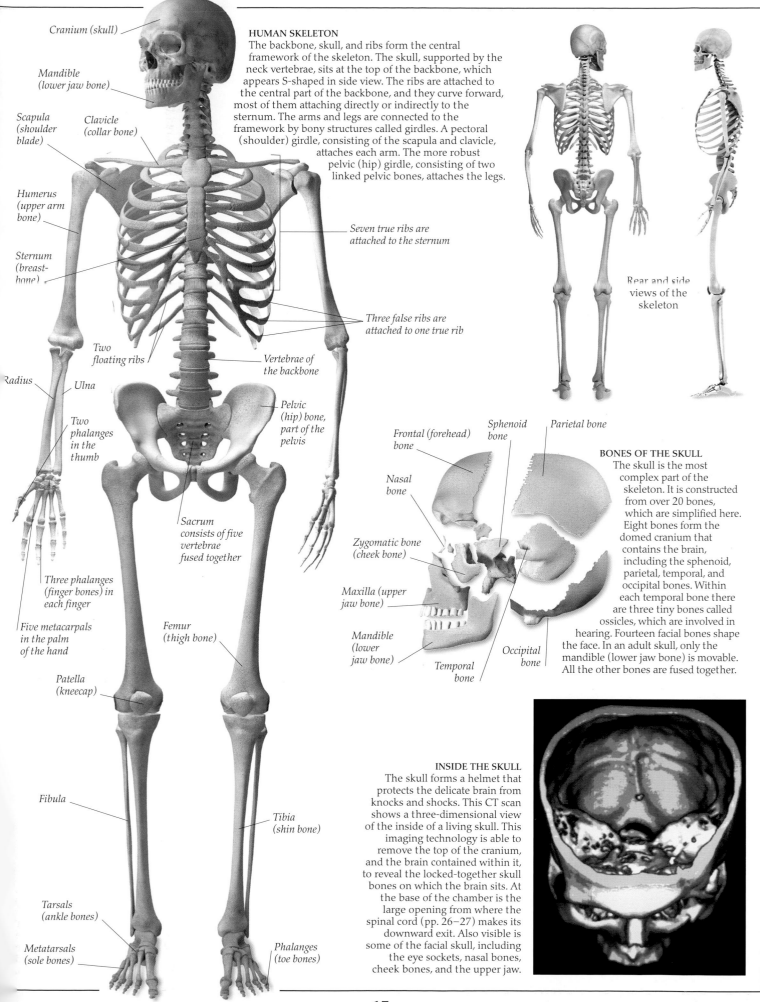

Cranium (skull)

Mandible (lower jaw bone)

Scapula (shoulder blade)

Clavicle (collar bone)

Humerus (upper arm bone)

Sternum (breast-bone)

Two floating ribs

Radius

Ulna

Two phalanges in the thumb

Three phalanges (finger bones) in each finger

Five metacarpals in the palm of the hand

Patella (kneecap)

Fibula

Tarsals (ankle bones)

Metatarsals (sole bones)

Femur (thigh bone)

Tibia (shin bone)

Phalanges (toe bones)

Pelvic (hip) bone, part of the pelvis

Sacrum consists of five vertebrae fused together

Vertebrae of the backbone

Three false ribs are attached to one true rib

Seven true ribs are attached to the sternum

HUMAN SKELETON

The backbone, skull, and ribs form the central framework of the skeleton. The skull, supported by the neck vertebrae, sits at the top of the backbone, which appears S-shaped in side view. The ribs are attached to the central part of the backbone, and they curve forward, most of them attaching directly or indirectly to the sternum. The arms and legs are connected to the framework by bony structures called girdles. A pectoral (shoulder) girdle, consisting of the scapula and clavicle, attaches each arm. The more robust pelvic (hip) girdle, consisting of two linked pelvic bones, attaches the legs.

Rear and side views of the skeleton

Frontal (forehead) bone

Sphenoid bone

Parietal bone

Nasal bone

Zygomatic bone (cheek bone)

Maxilla (upper jaw bone)

Mandible (lower jaw bone)

Temporal bone

Occipital bone

BONES OF THE SKULL

The skull is the most complex part of the skeleton. It is constructed from over 20 bones, which are simplified here. Eight bones form the domed cranium that contains the brain, including the sphenoid, parietal, temporal, and occipital bones. Within each temporal bone there are three tiny bones called ossicles, which are involved in hearing. Fourteen facial bones shape the face. In an adult skull, only the mandible (lower jaw bone) is movable. All the other bones are fused together.

INSIDE THE SKULL

The skull forms a helmet that protects the delicate brain from knocks and shocks. This CT scan shows a three-dimensional view of the inside of a living skull. This imaging technology is able to remove the top of the cranium, and the brain contained within it, to reveal the locked-together skull bones on which the brain sits. At the base of the chamber is the large opening from where the spinal cord (pp. 26–27) makes its downward exit. Also visible is some of the facial skull, including the eye sockets, nasal bones, cheek bones, and the upper jaw.

Inside bones

THE REMAINS OF EARLY HUMANS ON DISPLAY in museums might suggest that bones are simply dry, lifeless objects. However, inside the body, bones are moist, living organs with a complex structure of hard bone tissues, blood vessels, and nerves. Bone is as strong as steel, but only one-sixth its weight. Each bone also has a slight springiness that enables it to withstand knocks and jolts, usually without breaking. This extraordinary mix of attributes is due to its makeup. Bone tissue consists of tough, flexible collagen fibers—also found in tendons—wrapped around rock-hard mineral salts. Tough, dense bony tissue, called compact bone, forms just the outer layer of each bone. The inside is made of light-but-strong spongy bone. Without this interior, the bones of the skeleton would be far too heavy for the body to move.

GROWING BONE
In a young embryo the skeleton forms from bendy cartilage (p. 21). Over time, nuggets of bone, called ossification centers, develop within the cartilage. They grow and spread, turning cartilage into bone. This X-ray of a young child's hand shows growing bones (dark blue) and spaces where cartilage will be replaced.

Rope and pulley moves broken bones back into position

SETTING BONES
Bone setting is an ancient art. Some fossilized human skeletons of 100,000 years ago show that broken bones were set, or repositioned, to aid healing. Here, a 17th-century rope-and-pulley invention is pulling a broken arm bone back into place.

RESISTING PRESSURE
When weight is put on a bone, its structure prevents it from bending. For example, in the hip joint (shown here in cross-section) the head and neck of the femur (thigh bone) bear the full weight of the body. The largest area of bone consists of spongy bone, in which the trabeculae, or framework of struts, are lined up to resist downward force. The thin covering of compact bone is able to resist squashing on one side of the femur and stretching on the opposite side.

Pelvic (hip) bone

Head and neck of the femur (thigh bone)

Spongy bone

Compact bone resists squashing

Compact bone resists stretching

Muscle

INSIDE A LONG BONE
The cutaway below shows the structure of a long bone. Compact bone forms the hard outer layer. It is made up of parallel bundles of osteons (see opposite) that run lengthwise and act as weight-bearing pillars. Inside this is lighter spongy bone and a central, marrow-filled cavity. The periosteum, or outer skin, of the bone supplies its blood vessels.

SPONGY BONE
This SEM of spongy, or cancellous, bone shows an open framework of struts and spaces called trabeculae. In living bone the spaces are filled with bone marrow. Although trabeculae appear to be arranged in a haphazard way, they form a structure of great strength. Spongy bone is lighter than compact bone and so reduces the overall weight of a bone.

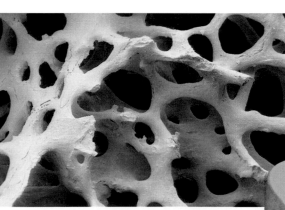

Head of bone is mostly spongy bone

Artery supplies oxygen-rich blood to the bone cells

BONE EXPERT

Giovanni Ingrassias (1510–80) was a founder of osteology, or the study of bones. He was a renowned physician and anatomy professor at Naples, Italy, and later at his birthplace, Palermo, in Sicily. His research corrected many mistaken ideas about bones. Ingrassias also identified the body's smallest bone, the stapes (stirrup) of the ear, and he described the arrangement of skull bones that form part of the eye socket.

BONE MICROSTRUCTURE

This model shows a microscopic view of a slice of compact bone. It is made up of osteons measuring just 0.01 in (0.25 mm) across. These consist of lamellae, or layered tubes, surrounding a central canal. Blood vessels run through the canal and supply food and oxygen to the osteocytes (bone cells). The osteocytes maintain the bone framework. This is made of flexible fiber of the protein collagen and hard mineral salts, mainly calcium phosphate. The combination of collagen and salts makes the bone lamellae strong but not brittle.

Osteon

Lamellae (layered tubes) of the osteon

Blood vessel

Outer lamellae strengthen the whole bone

Osteocyte (bone cell)

BONE CELLS

This SEM shows an osteocyte (bone cell) sitting in its lacuna—a tiny space in the framework of minerals and fibers that makes up compact bone. Although isolated, osteocytes are linked by strandlike extensions of their cell bodies that pass along the narrow canals inside bone.

Periosteum

Central canal of the osteon

Branch of blood vessel between the osteons

Spongy bone

Head of bone

Periosteum is the thin, fibrous membrane covering the entire bone surface

BONE MARROW

Jellylike bone marrow fills the spaces inside spongy bone as well as the central cavity of long bones. At birth, all of this marrow is red bone marrow, which produces new blood cells. These die rapidly and need to be replaced constantly. As the body grows, red marrow is gradually replaced by fat-storing yellow bone marrow. In adults, blood-cell-making red bone marrow remains only in a few bones, such as the skull, spine, and breastbone. These sites release over two million red blood cells per second into the bloodstream.

Compact bone is the hard, dense outer layer of the bone

Rich network of blood vessels nourishes the bone

Bone shaft

Osteon is one of the layered tubes that make up compact bone

Central cavity

Vein carries oxygen-poor blood away from the bone cells

Yellow bone marrow fills the central cavity and stores fat

MAKING NEW BLOOD CELLS

This SEM shows red bone marrow, where hemopoiesis (the making of blood cells) takes place. Unspecialized stem cells multiply to produce cells destined to become blood cells (p. 46). These cells divide and their offspring mature rapidly to form billions of red blood cells (red) and white blood cells (blue).

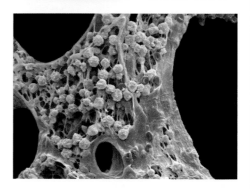

Joints between bones

W HEREVER TWO OR MORE BONES meet in the skeleton, they form a joint. The majority of the body's 400-plus joints, such as those found in the fingers and toes, are freely movable. Without them, the body would be rigid and unable to jump, catch a ball, write, or perform any of the incredible variety of movements of which it is capable. There are several different types of movable joint. The range of movement each permits depends on the shapes of the bone ends that meet in that joint. Joints are held together by ligaments and contain cartilage. This is a tough tissue that also supports other structures around the body.

Condyloid joint allows the head to nod

Pivot joint allows the head to shake

Hinge joint allows the arm to bend at the elbow

SUPPLE JOINTS
Like any body part, joints benefit from use, and deteriorate with neglect. Activities such as yoga promote the full range of joint movement, encourage maximum flexibility, and help to postpone the stiffness, pain, or discomfort that can sometimes arrive with the onset of old age.

Simple hinge joints between the phalanges (finger bones) enable the fingers to bend in two places

Condyloid joint is an oval ball-and-socket joint allowing the fingers to swivel, but not to rotate

Palm of hand extends to the knuckles

Gliding joints allow limited sliding movements between the eight bones of the wrist

Saddle joint gives thumb great flexibility and a delicate touch when picking up tiny objects with the fingers

Limb can move in many directions

Femur (thigh bone)

Pelvic (hip) bone

Ball-and-socket joint in the hip

BALLS, SOCKETS, AND HINGES
The hip and knee provide perfect examples of joints in action. Their different movements can be seen whenever someone climbs, walks, dances, or kicks. The hip joint is a ball-and-socket joint. The rounded end of the thigh bone swivels in the cup-shaped socket in the hip bone and permits movement in all directions, including rotation. The knee is a hinge joint. It has a more limited movement, mainly in one front-to-back direction.

Femur (thigh bone)

Tibia (shin bone)

Hinge joint in the knee

Limb moves back and forth in one direction

Gliding joint allows the kneecap to move away from the femur (thigh bone) as the knee bends

Gliding joint between the fibula and tibia (shin bone) allows small movements of the fibula

Hinge joint allows the foot to bend at the ankle

JOINTS GALORE
With its 27 bones and 19 movable joints, the hand is amazingly flexible and able to perform many delicate tasks. The first knuckle joint of each digit (finger) is condyloid, which together with the other hinge joints enables the fingers to curl around and grasp objects. The saddle joint at the base of the thumb—the most mobile digit—allows it to swing across the palm and touch the tips of the other fingers. This ability allows the hands to perform many tasks, from threading a needle to lifting heavy weights.

VERSATILE MOVER
The skeleton is an extremely flexible framework. This is because it contains many different types of joint, each permitting different ranges of movement. Some, such as ball-and-socket, condyloid, or saddle joints, allow flexible movements in several directions. Others are more limited, such as pivot joints that allow one bone to turn on another from side to side. Hinge joints simply move back and forth, and gliding joints enable small sliding movements between bones.

BINDING THE BONES

Tough straps of strong, elastic tissue called ligaments surround bone ends in a joint and bind them together. In the foot, a number of ligaments hold together the tarsals and metatarsals (ankle and sole bones) in the ankle joint. Ligaments hold the bones securely against one another, and prevent them from moving excessively.

Tibia (shin bone)

Fibula

Ligament linking the tibia and fibula

Ligament linking the calcaneus and fibula

Calcaneus (heel bone)

Pivot joint permits the forearm to twist

Gliding joint between the rib and backbone

Saddle joint gives the thumb great mobility

Condyloid joint gives the wrist flexibility

Metatarsals (sole bones)

Tarsals (ankle bones)

Ligaments connecting the tarsals and metatarsals

Ball and socket joint between the femur (thigh bone) and hip enables the leg to move in all directions

Hinge joint allows the leg to bend at the knee

Gliding joint between the tarsals (ankle bones) allows little movement, which strengthens the ankle

Condyloid joint allows the toes to bend and wiggle

Hinge joint allows the toe to bend

INSIDE A SYNOVIAL JOINT

Most joints are synovial (freely moving) joints. This view into a typical synovial joint shows its main parts. Inside the protective joint capsule and ligaments is the synovial membrane. This makes slippery synovial fluid, the oil that lubricates the joint. The bone ends are covered by friction-reducing, shiny hyaline cartilage. Like a sponge, this soaks up synovial fluid, releasing it when put under pressure, enabling the joint to move smoothly.

Bone marrow

Bone

Joint capsule

Synovial membrane

Synovial fluid

Hyaline cartilage

Ligaments

Cartilage

Tough and flexible, cartilage is a supporting tissue that resists pushing and pulling forces. There are three types of cartilage in the body—hyaline, elastic, and fibrocartilage. Hyaline cartilage covers the ends of bones to help joints move smoothly (see above). It also supports the tip of the nose, larynx (voice box) and trachea (windpipe), and connects the ribs to the sternum (breast bone). Elastic cartilage is strong and flexible. It supports the outside of the ear and also the epiglottis—the flap that stops food from going down the wrong way into the trachea. Fibrocartilage can withstand heavy pressure and is found in the disks between vertebrae in the backbone. It also forms the padlike cartilages, called menisci, that act as shock absorbers in the knee joints.

CARTILAGE CELLS

Cartilage-making cells are called chondrocytes. They live buried in the cartilage that they make around themselves. This is composed of fibers of the tough protein collagen and fibers of the elastic protein elastin. They are woven together into a stiff jelly with water. Cartilage has a limited blood supply. Nutrients seep into cartilage cells from the blood vessels that run around its edges.

Chondrocyte

KNEE TROUBLE

The knee is the body's biggest joint. It is strengthened by ligaments inside the joint, and cushioned from jolts by the menisci. Sports such as soccer involve rapid turns and high kicks. These can cause knee injuries for regular players such as Brazil's Ronaldo. Common injuries include tears to ligaments or menisci.

The body's muscles

MUSCLE IS A BODY TISSUE THAT HAS A UNIQUE ABILITY to pull and generate movement by contracting, or getting shorter. Skeletal muscles, which make up nearly half the body's total mass, cover the skeleton and are attached to its bones. These muscles shape the body, hold it upright to maintain posture, and, by pulling on bones, allow it to perform a wide range of movements from blinking to running. Most muscles are given Latin names that describe their location, size, shape, or action. For example, the adductor longus is long and it adducts the leg, or pulls it toward the body. This naming practice dates from before the 17th century, when scientists such as Niels Stensen and Giorgio Baglivi were undertaking their pioneering research. The two other muscle types in the body are smooth muscle and cardiac muscle.

MUSCLES UNDER THE MICROSCOPE
Danish scientist and bishop Niels Stensen (1638–86) studied in Denmark and the Netherlands. He conducted microscopic work on muscles and discovered that their contraction was due to the combined shortening of the thousands of tiny fibers that make up each muscle.

THE ULTIMATE BOOK
Italian anatomist Giorgio Baglivi (1668–1707) told his students: "You will never find a more interesting, more instructive book than the patient himself." He was the first to note that skeletal muscles are different from the muscles working the intestines and other organs.

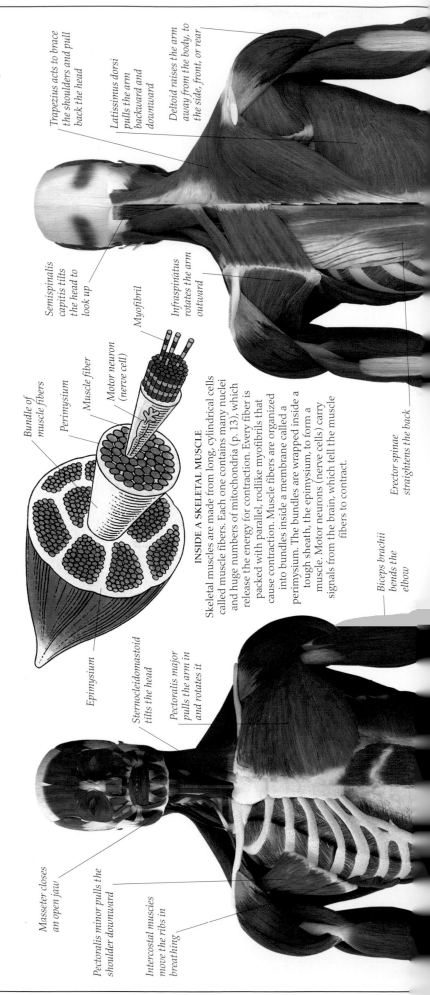

Trapezius acts to brace the shoulders and pull back the head

Latissimus dorsi pulls the arm backward and downward

Deltoid raises the arm away from the body, to the side, front, or rear

Semispinalis capitis tilts the head to look up

Infraspinatus rotates the arm outward

Myofibril

Bundle of muscle fibers

Perimysium

Muscle fiber

Motor neuron (nerve cell)

Epimysium

Sternocleidomastoid tilts the head

Pectoralis major pulls the arm in and rotates it

INSIDE A SKELETAL MUSCLE
Skeletal muscles are made from long, cylindrical cells called muscle fibers. Each one contains many nuclei and huge numbers of mitochondria (p. 13), which release the energy for contraction. Every fiber is packed with parallel, rodlike myofibrils that cause contraction. Muscle fibers are organized into bundles inside a membrane called a perimysium. The bundles are wrapped inside a tough sheath, the epimysium, to form a muscle. Motor neurons (nerve cells) carry signals from the brain, which tell the muscle fibers to contract.

Biceps brachii bends the elbow

Erector spinae straightens the back

Masseter closes an open jaw

Pectoralis minor pulls the shoulder downward

Intercostal muscles move the ribs in breathing

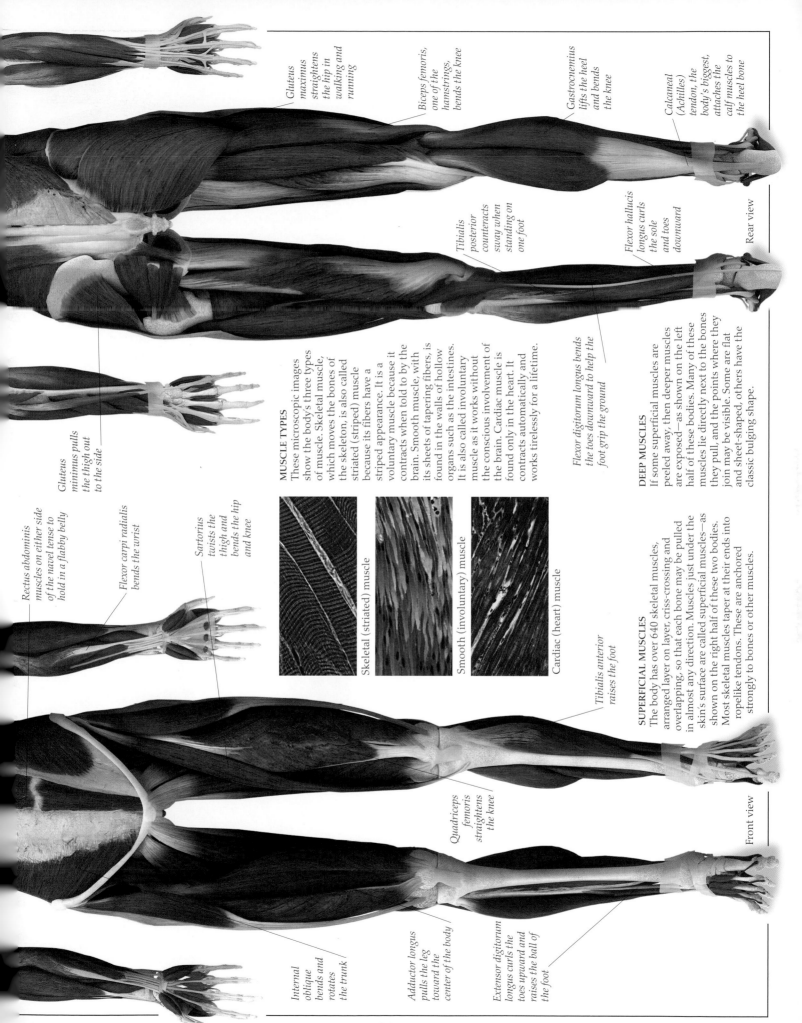

Gluteus maximus straightens the hip in walking and running

Biceps femoris, one of the hamstrings, bends the knee

Gastrocnemius lifts the heel and bends the knee

Calcaneal (Achilles) tendon, the body's biggest, attaches the calf muscles to the heel bone

Tibialis posterior counteracts sway when standing on one foot

Flexor hallucis longus curls the sole and toes downward

Rear view

Gluteus minimus pulls the thigh out to the side

Flexor digitorum longus bends the toes downward to help the foot grip the ground

MUSCLE TYPES

These microscopic images show the body's three types of muscle. Skeletal muscle, which moves the bones of the skeleton, is also called striated (striped) muscle because its fibers have a striped appearance. It is a voluntary muscle because it contracts when told to by the brain. Smooth muscle, with its sheets of tapering fibers, is found in the walls of hollow organs such as the intestines. It is also called involuntary muscle as it works without the conscious involvement of the brain. Cardiac muscle is found only in the heart. It contracts automatically and works tirelessly for a lifetime.

DEEP MUSCLES

If some superficial muscles are peeled away, then deeper muscles are exposed—as shown on the left half of these bodies. Many of these muscles lie directly next to the bones they pull, and the points where they join may be visible. Some are flat and sheet-shaped, others have the classic bulging shape.

Skeletal (striated) muscle

Smooth (involuntary) muscle

Cardiac (heart) muscle

SUPERFICIAL MUSCLES

The body has over 640 skeletal muscles, arranged layer on layer, criss-crossing and overlapping, so that each bone may be pulled in almost any direction. Muscles just under the skin's surface are called superficial muscles—as shown on the right half of these two bodies. Most skeletal muscles taper at their ends into ropelike tendons. These are anchored strongly to bones or other muscles.

Rectus abdominis muscles on either side of the navel tense to hold in a flabby belly

Flexor carpi radialis bends the wrist

Sartorius twists the thigh and bends the hip and knee

Tibialis anterior raises the foot

Internal oblique bends and rotates the trunk

Adductor longus pulls the leg toward the center of the body

Extensor digitorum longus curls the toes upward and raises the ball of the foot

Quadriceps femoris straightens the knee

Front view

23

The moving body

THE SKELETAL MUSCLES MOVE THE BODY in many ways, enabling us to smile, nod, walk, and jump. Muscles are attached to bones by tough, fibrous cords called tendons, and they extend across the movable joints between bones. When muscles contract (get shorter), they pull on a bone and movement is produced. The bone that moves when the muscle contracts is called the insertion and the other bone, which stays still, is called the origin. For example, the biceps muscle in the upper arm has its origin in the shoulder blade and its insertion in the radius, a forearm bone. Muscles can only pull, not push, so moving a body part in different directions requires opposing pairs of muscles. In addition to moving the body, certain muscles in the neck, back, and legs tense (partially contract) to maintain posture and keep the body balanced.

THE THREE S-WORDS
Muscle fitness can be assessed by three S-words: strength, stamina, and suppleness. Some activities develop only one factor, but other exercises, such as swimming and dancing, promote all three.

Neck muscles bend the head back

Muscles in the back of the forearm extend (straighten) the fingers

Back muscles arch the back

Extensor tendon to the index finger

Phalanges (finger bones)

Transverse ligament stops the tendons from moving sideways

Biceps contracted

Triceps relaxed

Triceps contracted

Raised forearm

Flexed elbow

Biceps relaxed

Extensor retinaculum is the band that holds the long tendons in place

Separate extensor tendons begin at the end of the extensor digitorum

MUSCLE PAIRS
Muscles can only contract and pull—they cannot push. To move a body part in opposite directions requires two different muscles. Many muscles are arranged in opposing pairs. For example, in the arm the biceps pulls the forearm upward and bends the elbow, while its opposing partner, the triceps, pulls the forearm downward and straightens the elbow. Most body movements result from the opposing actions of muscle teams.

Elbow straight

Forearm lowered

Extensor digitorum straightens the fingers when it contracts

TENDONS
Many of the muscles that move the fingers are not in the hand at all, but in the forearm. They work the fingers by remote control, using long tendons extending from the ends of the muscles to attach to the bones that they move. The tendons run smoothly in slippery tendon sheaths that reduce wear. Tendons, wherever they occur in the body, attach muscles to the bones that they pull on.

POWER AND PRECISION
The incredible precision of the fingers is due to muscles working the flexible framework of 27 bones in each hand—and a lifetime of practice. Pianists can train their brains to coordinate complex, rhythmic movements in all 10 fingers, while the notes they play range from delicate to explosive.

WORKING TOGETHER

For this young gymnast to perform a pose called an arabesque requires a considerable feat of coordination. Areas of the brain that control movement and balance send out nerve signals to instruct specific skeletal muscles when to contract and by how much. Muscles in the hands, arms, torso, and legs work together to put the gymnast in this position. Signals from the muscles and tendons also feed back to the brain so that minor adjustments can be made to maintain her balance.

Calf muscles bend the foot downward to point the toes

Hand muscles pull the fingers together

Muscles at the back of the thigh pull the leg backward

Muscle at the front of the thigh pulls the leg forward and straightens the knee

Pairs of muscles at the front and back of the leg tense to keep balance

SWAMMERDAM OF AMSTERDAM

Dutch physician Jan Swammerdam (1637–90) researched muscle contraction. At the time it was believed that a vital spirit passed along nerves and inflated muscles to make them contract. Swammerdam showed that this was not the case, and that muscles altered in shape, but not in volume (the space they take up) during contraction.

MYOFIBRIL CONTRACTION

This TEM shows myofibrils, the long cylinders that extend the length of a skeletal muscle fiber, or cell. These myofibrils are running from left to right. They are divided into units, which sit between the thin, vertical lines. Each unit contains thick and thin filaments, which are overlapping to produce the blue-and-pink pattern. As muscles contract, the thick and thin filaments slide over each other, making the myofibril shorter. This shortens the entire muscle.

Frontalis raises the eyebrows and wrinkles the forehead

Orbicularis oculi closes the eye

Corrugator supercilii pulls the eyebrows together

Levator labii superioris lifts and curls the upper lip

Orbicularis oris closes, purses, and protrudes the lips—during a kiss, for example

Mentalis protrudes the lower lip

Depressor anguli oris pulls down the corner of the mouth

Temporalis lifts the lower jaw, during biting, for example

FACE, HEAD, AND NECK

From frowning to smiling, around 30 facial muscles produce the great variety of expressions that reveal how a person is feeling. These muscles are also involved in activities such as chewing, blinking, and yawning. Facial muscles work by joining the skull bones to different areas of skin, which are tugged as the muscles contract. The head is supported and moved by muscles that start at the backbone, shoulder blades, and bones in the upper chest. These pass through the neck and attach to the base of the skull.

Zygomatic muscles raise the corners of the mouth upward

Risorius pulls the corner of the mouth in a smile

Sternocleidomastoid tilts the head forward or to one side

Trapezius pulls the head upright

The nervous system

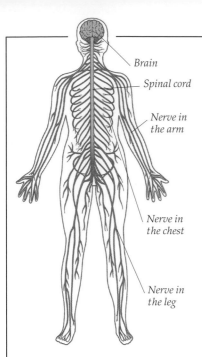

- Brain
- Spinal cord
- Nerve in the arm
- Nerve in the chest
- Nerve in the leg

WITHOUT THE CONTROL AND COORDINATION of its nervous system, the body could not function. With split-second timing, the nervous system allows a person to feel, see, and hear, to move, and to think and remember—all at the same time. It also automatically controls many internal body processes. Together, the brain and spinal cord form the central nervous system (CNS). This links to the body through a network of nerves. The nervous system is constructed from billions of interconnected neurons. These are specialized cells that carry electrical signals at lightning-fast speeds of up to 100 metres per second (328 ft/s). Sensory neurons carry signals from the sense organs (pp. 32–39) to the CNS. Motor neurons carry instructions from the CNS to the muscles, and association neurons process signals within the CNS itself.

NERVE NETWORK
The brain and spinal cord form the control center of the nervous system with its cablelike network of nerves. Nerves are bundles of neurons. The bundles divide to reach every nook and cranny of a body's tissues. Laid end to end, a body's nerves would wrap around the Earth twice.

Facial nerve controls the muscles of facial expression

PAVLOV'S PERFORMING DOGS
A reflex is an automatic reaction to a particular stimulus, or trigger. For example, dogs, like people, naturally salivate (drool) at the sight and smell of food. Russian scientist Ivan Pavlov (1849–1936) trained some dogs to associate feeding time with the sound of a bell. In time, the dogs drooled when hearing the bell alone. Pavlov called this learned response a "conditioned reflex" to distinguish it from a natural, built-in reflex.

CRANIAL AND SPINAL NERVES
The operations of the brain—the cerebrum, cerebellum, and brain stem—and the spinal cord depend on a constant flow of incoming and outgoing signals. These arrive and depart through twelve pairs of cranial nerves that start in the brain, and 31 pairs of spinal nerves that start in the spinal cord. Each nerve has sensory neurons, which carry sensations from a body area to the brain, and motor neurons, which carry instructions from the brain to move muscles in that same body area. The sympathetic ganglion chain is part of the autonomic nervous system. This automatically controls vital processes that we are unaware of, such as the body's heart rate.

Trigeminal nerve branch supplies the upper teeth and cheek

Brachial plexus leads to the nerves that supply the arm and hand

Ulnar nerve controls the muscles that bend the wrist and fingers

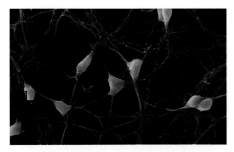

BRANCHES EVERYWHERE
This microscopic view shows association neurons in the brain. Each neuron may have branching connections with thousands or tens of thousands of other neurons, forming a massive communication network. Nerve signals can take any path between neurons, and the number of routes are countless.

Intercostal nerve controls the muscles between the ribs

Cerebrum
processes
and stores
information

Cerebellum
controls
movement
and balance

Axon bundle carries signals
to and from the brain

Spinal nerve

Front root carries
outgoing signals

Back root carries
incoming signals

Gray matter
contains neuron
cell bodies

White matter
consists of
axon bundles

Meninges are
three
protective
membranes

Brain stem
controls the
heart rate and
breathing

Spinal cord
relays signals
between the
spinal nerves
and the brain

Sympathetic
ganglion chain
controls automatic
functions

Spinal nerves are
arranged in pairs

Phrenic nerve
supplies the
diaphragm, the
muscle that
causes breathing

Vagus nerve
helps control
the heart rate

FOUNDER OF NEUROLOGY
French physician Jean-Martin
Charcot (1825–93) was a pioneer of
neurology, the study of nervous
system diseases. He recognized
several important diseases, including
multiple sclerosis, a disabling
condition caused by damage to the
brain and spinal cord. He also
contributed to the development of
psychiatry, the branch of medicine
that deals with mental illness.

THE SPINAL CORD
No thicker than a finger, the spinal cord (shown here
in a cross-section) is a downward extension of the
brain. The spinal cord relays nerve signals between
the spinal nerves and the brain. Each spinal nerve has
two roots. One contains sensory neurons bringing
incoming signals from sense receptors, such as those
involved with taste, hearing, or touch. The other
contains motor neurons carrying outgoing signals to
the muscles. The spinal cord also controls many
automatic body reflexes, such as pulling the hand
away from a hot or sharp object.

NEURON STRUCTURE
A neuron consists of a nerve cell
body with many short, branched
endings called dendrites and one
long axon, or nerve fiber. Dendrites
receive nerve signals from other
neurons across junctions called
synapses. Axons carry nerve signals
away from the cell body and form
synapses with other neurons, or
with muscles. In many neurons, the
axon is insulated with a fatty, myelin
sheath. This increases the speed of
signals traveling along a neuron.

Neuron's cell
body contains
its nucleus

Part of
another
neuron

Synapse
between
two
neurons

Dendrite

Axon
(nerve fiber)

Longest axon
is up to 3 ft
(1 m) long

Insulating
myelin sheath

The brain

THE BRAIN IS THE BODY'S most complex organ and the nervous system's control center. It contains 100 billion neurons (nerve cells), each linked to hundreds or thousands of other neurons, which together form a massive communication network with incredible processing power. The cerebrum, the main part of the brain, processes and stores incoming information and sends out instructions to the body. These tasks, from thinking and reasoning to seeing and feeling, are carried out by the cerebral cortex, the thin, folded outer layer of the cerebrum. Over the past 150 years, scientists have mapped the cerebral cortex and discovered which tasks are carried out by different parts of the brain.

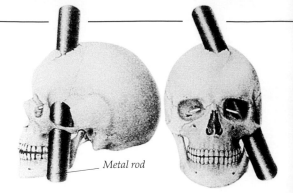

Metal rod

HOLE IN THE HEAD
Phineas Gage was the foreman of a quarrying gang in the US. In 1848, a gunpowder accident blew a metal rod through his cheek, up through the left frontal lobe of his brain, and out of his skull. Gage survived and the wound healed, but his personality changed from contented and considerate, to obstinate, moody, and foul-mouthed. He was living proof that the front of the brain is involved in aspects of personality.

THE BRAIN FROM BELOW
The brain has three main parts. The cerebrum dominates the brain and makes up 85 percent of its weight. The brain stem consists of the pons, medulla oblongata, and midbrain (see p. 30). It relays signals between the cerebrum and the spinal cord, and controls automatic functions, such as breathing and the heart rate. The cerebellum is responsible for controlling balance and posture, and for producing coordinated movements.

Left hemisphere of cerebrum controls the right side of the body

Olfactory bulb carries signals from the nose to the brain

Optic nerve (shown cut) carries signals from the eyes to the brain

Pons is the middle part of the brain stem

LEFT AND RIGHT
Nerve fibers in the brain stem cross from left to right and from right to left. This means that the right hemisphere (half) of the cerebrum receives sensory input from, and controls the movements of, the left side of the body, and vice versa. The right side of the brain also handles face recognition, and creative abilities such as music, while the left side controls language, problem solving, and mathematical skills. Usually the left hemisphere dominates, which is why most people are right handed. Left-handed people, such as rock guitarist Jimi Hendrix (1942–70), often excel in the creative arts and music.

Right hemisphere of the cerebrum controls the left side of the body

Medulla oblongata is part of the brain stem that controls breathing and the heart rate

Cerebellum controls body movements

Spinal cord (shown cut) relays the nerve signals between the brain and body

SITE OF SPEECH
French physician Paul Pierre Broca (1824–80) discovered which area of the brain controls speech. Broca had a male patient with a limited ability to speak. After the patient's death in 1861, Broca examined his brain and found a damaged patch on the left cerebrum. He concluded that the area, later called Broca's area, coordinated the muscles of the larynx and mouth, which are used for speaking.

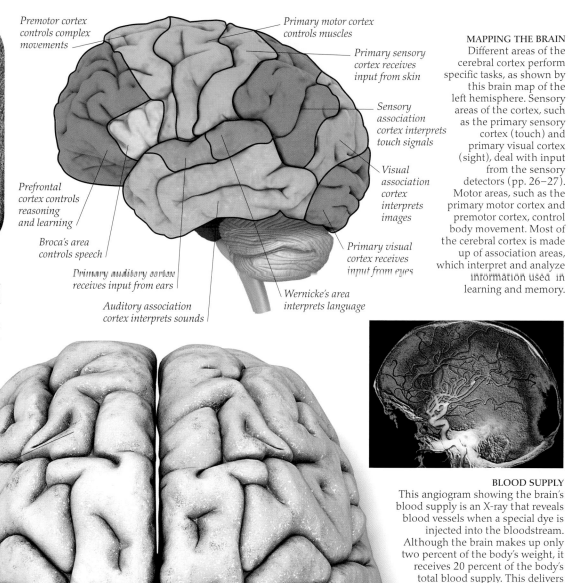

Premotor cortex controls complex movements

Primary motor cortex controls muscles

Primary sensory cortex receives input from skin

Sensory association cortex interprets touch signals

Visual association cortex interprets images

Prefrontal cortex controls reasoning and learning

Broca's area controls speech

Primary auditory cortex receives input from ears

Auditory association cortex interprets sounds

Wernicke's area interprets language

Primary visual cortex receives input from eyes

MAPPING THE BRAIN
Different areas of the cerebral cortex perform specific tasks, as shown by this brain map of the left hemisphere. Sensory areas of the cortex, such as the primary sensory cortex (touch) and primary visual cortex (sight), deal with input from the sensory detectors (pp. 26–27). Motor areas, such as the primary motor cortex and premotor cortex, control body movement. Most of the cerebral cortex is made up of association areas, which interpret and analyze information used in learning and memory.

Frontal lobe at the front of the cerebral hemisphere

Left cerebral hemisphere

Temporal lobe at the side of the cerebral hemisphere

Parietal lobe on the rear top section of the cerebral hemisphere

Occipital lobe at the back of the cerebral hemisphere

Longitudinal fissure separates the two cerebral hemispheres

Gyrus (ridge)

Right cerebral hemisphere

Sulcus (groove)

BLOOD SUPPLY
This angiogram showing the brain's blood supply is an X-ray that reveals blood vessels when a special dye is injected into the bloodstream. Although the brain makes up only two percent of the body's weight, it receives 20 percent of the body's total blood supply. This delivers the oxygen and glucose (sugar) that the brain requires to function normally.

THE BRAIN FROM ABOVE
The surface layer of the cerebrum, called the cerebral cortex, is heavily folded with gyri (ridges) and sulci (grooves). These folds greatly increase the surface area of cerebral cortex that can fit inside the skull. If laid out flat, the cerebral cortex would cover about the same area as a pillow. The deepest groove, the longitudinal fissure, divides the cerebrum into the right and left hemispheres. Deep grooves divide each hemisphere into four areas, called the frontal, temporal, parietal, and occipital lobes.

Inside the brain

A LOOK INSIDE THE BRAIN REVEALS even more about its structure and workings than the view from the outside. Deep inside the brain, beneath the cerebrum, the thalamus acts as a relay station for incoming nerve signals, and the hypothalamus automatically controls a vast array of body activities. Also unseen from the outside, the limbic system is the emotional center of the brain, dealing with instincts, fears, and feelings. Inside the cerebrum there are linked chambers called ventricles that are filled with a liquid called cerebrospinal fluid (CSF). CSF is produced by blood and circulates through the ventricles, helping to feed the brain cells. Although scientists now know much about the brain's structure, they have yet to fully understand how we think and why we dream.

LIQUID INTELLIGENCE
In ancient times, intelligence and other mental abilities were said to be generated by a mystical animal spirit that filled the ventricles of the brain. This 17th-century illustration links each ventricle with a mental quality such as imagination. Today's scientists link the brain's abilities to various regions of its solid parts.

MATTERS OF THE MIND
Austrian physician Sigmund Freud (1856–1939) was one of the pioneers of psychiatry, a branch of medicine that deals with mental disorders. He developed psychoanalysis, a therapy that attempts to treat mental illness by investigating the unconscious mind. Since Freud's time, psychiatrists have made great progress in linking mental disorders to abnormalities of the brain structure or its biochemical workings.

Thalamus relays nerve signals to the cerebrum

Inner surface of the left cerebral hemisphere

Corpus callosum (band of nerve fibers) connects the left and right cerebral hemispheres

Midbrain is at the top of the brain stem

Ventricle contains cerebrospinal fluid to feed the brain cells

Hypothalamus controls many automatic activities including blood pressure, hunger, and sleep

Pituitary gland (pp. 40–41)

Cerebellum controls muscle movement and balance

Medulla oblongata is the lowest part of the brain stem

Pons is in the middle of the brain stem

Spinal cord (shown cut)

LOOKING INSIDE THE BRAIN
This side-on model shows the inner surface of the left cerebrum and the inner parts of the brain in cross-section. The thalamus sits in the center of the brain and relays signals to the cerebrum. The cerebellum is positioned at the back of the brain, along with the midbrain, pons, and medulla oblongata, which make up the brain stem.

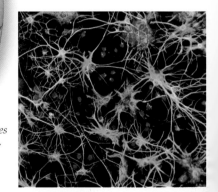

SUPPORT CELLS
Over 90 percent of cells in the nervous system are not neurons (nerve cells) but glial, or support, cells. This microscopic image shows astrocytes, a type of glial cell found in the cerebral cortex. Astrocytes help to supply neurons with nutrients. Other functions of glial cells include destroying bacteria and forming the insulating sheath around axons (nerve fibers).

DEEP THOUGHT
French sculptor Auguste Rodin (1840–1917) portrayed deep concentration in his statue *The Thinker*. When people want to think seriously about a matter, they stare into space, almost unseeing, enabling them to concentrate on their thought processes.

Cingulate gyrus deals with emotions

Fornix is the pathway that links different parts of the limbic system

Hippocampus deals with memory and navigation

Parahippocampal gyrus deals with anger and fright, and recalls memories

Mamillary body relays signals from the amygdala and hippocampus to the thalamus

Amygdala assesses danger and triggers feelings of fear

THE LIMBIC SYSTEM
This curve of linked structures, called the limbic system, is located on the inner surface of each cerebral hemisphere and around the top of the brain stem. It deals with emotions such as pleasure, anger, hope, and disappointment. It makes us frightened and aware of danger, and helps us to store memories. The sense of smell is also linked to the limbic system, which explains why certain odors can arouse feelings and bring back memories.

Olfactory bulbs carry signals from the smell receptors in the nose directly to the limbic system

SWEET DREAMS
French artist Henri Rousseau (1844–1910) painted unreal, dreamlike scenes in many of his works, such as the musician dreaming about a lion in *The Sleeping Gypsy*. When people sleep, many have dreams in which real or familiar experiences are mixed up with strange happenings. One explanation for this might be that when we sleep, the brain replays recent experiences at random and stores significant events in the memory. Dreaming is a side effect of this brain activity.

White matter of cerebrum consists of axons encased in insulating sheaths

Cerebral cortex consists of gray matter

Longitudinal fissure separates the left and right cerebral hemispheres

Fornix is the nerve pathway that links parts of the limbic system

Corpus callosum (band of nerve fibers)

Basal nuclei are deep areas of gray matter that control body movement

Thalamus relays incoming signals to the cerebral cortex

Ventricle

GRAY AND WHITE MATTER
This vertical cross-section gives a front view of the parts of the cerebrum. The cerebral cortex (surface layer of the brain) is made up of gray matter. This consists of neuron cell bodies, dendrites, and short axons (p. 27). White matter consists of longer axons, which join parts of the cerebral cortex together, or connect the brain to the rest of the nervous system. Basal nuclei are deep areas of gray matter that control body movement.

Pons

Cerebellum

Spinal cord

Medulla oblongata

MIND OVER MATTER
Scientists continue to investigate puzzling features of the human brain. Some hope to prove that the workings of the mind cannot always be measured or described in terms of nerve signals or chemical processes. They believe that techniques such as meditation (deep thinking), performed here by a Buddhist monk, can carry the mind beyond the physical boundaries of the body.

Skin and touch

Uɴʟɪᴋᴇ ᴛʜᴇ ᴏᴛʜᴇʀ ꜱᴇɴꜱᴇ ᴏʀɢᴀɴꜱ, such as the eyes, skin is not simply involved with a single sense. In addition to its role in the sense of touch, it has many other jobs. Skin is the body's largest organ. On an adult, this living, leathery overcoat weighs about 11 lb (5 kg). The skin's tough surface layer, called the epidermis, keeps out water, dust, germs, and harmful ultraviolet rays from the Sun. It continually replaces itself to repair wear and tear. Beneath the epidermis lies a thicker layer, called the dermis, which is packed with sensory receptors, nerves, and blood vessels. In hot conditions, the dermis also helps steady body temperature at 98.6°F (37°C) by releasing cooling sweat from its sweat glands. Hair and nails grow from the skin's epidermis and provide additional body covering and protection.

COOLING THE BODY
This SEM shows one of about three million sweat pores in the skin's surface. Sweat glands in the dermis produce a salty liquid, called sweat. When the body is too hot, more sweat flows through the pores onto the skin's surface and then evaporates. This process draws heat from the body and cools it down.

FINGERTIP READING
The Braille system enables people with sight problems to read using the sense of touch. It uses patterns of raised dots to represent letters and numbers, which are felt through the sensitive fingertips. The system was devised in 1824 by French teenager Louis Braille (1809–52), who was blinded at three years old.

Ridges on fingertips aid grip (see opposite)

GET A GRIP
The skin on the palm of the hand is covered with ridges. These help the hand to grip objects when performing different tasks. Beneath the palm is a triangle-shaped sheet of tough, meshed fibers called the palmar aponeurosis. This anchors the skin and stops it from sliding over the underlying fat and muscle.

Lines on the palm of the hand

UNDER YOUR SKIN
The upper surface layers of the epidermis consist of flat, interlocking dead cells. These are filled with hard-wearing protein called keratin. The skin flakes as dead cells wear away and are replaced with new cells. New cells are produced by cell division (p. 62) in the lowest layer of the epidermis. The thicker dermis layer contains the sense receptors that help the body detect changes in touch, temperature, vibration, pressure, and pain. The dermis also houses coiled sweat glands and hair follicles. The sebaceous glands release oily sebum, which keeps the skin and hair soft and flexible.

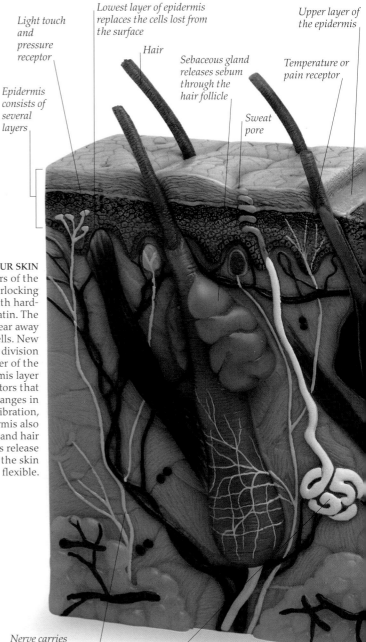

Light touch and pressure receptor

Epidermis consists of several layers

Lowest layer of epidermis replaces the cells lost from the surface

Hair

Sebaceous gland releases sebum through the hair follicle

Sweat pore

Upper layer of the epidermis

Temperature or pain receptor

Nerve carries signals to the brain

Sweat gland

Loop pattern on fingerprint

FINGERPRINTS

The skin covering the fingers, toes, palms, and soles, is folded into swirling patterns of tiny ridges. The ridges help the skin of the hands and feet to grip, aided by sweat released through sweat pores, which open along the crest of each ridge. When fingers touch smooth surfaces, such as glass, their ridges leave behind sweaty patterns called fingerprints. These are classified into types by the presence of three main features: arches, loops, and whorls. Each human has a unique set of fingerprints.

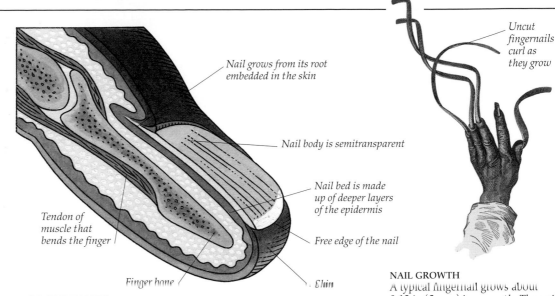

Nail grows from its root embedded in the skin

Nail body is semitransparent

Nail bed is made up of deeper layers of the epidermis

Free edge of the nail

Tendon of muscle that bends the finger

Finger bone

Skin

Uncut fingernails curl as they grow

INSENSITIVE NAILS

Nails are the protective covers at the ends of fingers and toes. They are hard extensions of the epidermis, made from dead cells filled with keratin. This is why nails, like hair, can be trimmed without feeling pain. Each nail has a free edge, a body, and a root embedded in the skin. The nail grows from new cells produced in the root. These push the nail forward, sliding it over the nail bed as it grows.

NAIL GROWTH

A typical fingernail grows about 0.12 in (3 mm) in a month. The nails on the longer fingers grow faster than those on the shorter ones. Fingernails also grow faster in the summer months than in winter. Toenails grow three or four times more slowly. If left uncut, fingernails can reach a yard or more in length.

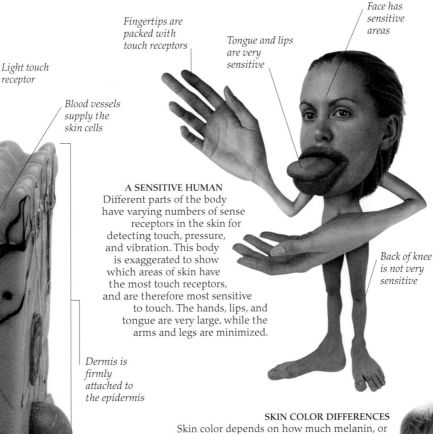

Hair follicle contains the growing hair

Light touch receptor

Blood vessels supply the skin cells

Fingertips are packed with touch receptors

Tongue and lips are very sensitive

Face has sensitive areas

A SENSITIVE HUMAN

Different parts of the body have varying numbers of sense receptors in the skin for detecting touch, pressure, and vibration. This body is exaggerated to show which areas of skin have the most touch receptors, and are therefore most sensitive to touch. The hands, lips, and tongue are very large, while the arms and legs are minimized.

Back of knee is not very sensitive

Dermis is firmly attached to the epidermis

Pressure and vibration receptor

Fat layer under the dermis insulates the body

DEAD HAIRS

This SEM shows hair shafts in the skin. Hair grows from living cells at the base of the follicle. As the cells push upward, they fill with keratin and die. Millions of short, fine hairs cover much of the body, except for palms of the hands, soles of the feet, and lips. Longer, thicker hairs grow on the scalp to protect it from harmful sunlight and prevent heat loss.

SKIN COLOR DIFFERENCES

Skin color depends on how much melanin, or brown pigment (coloring), it contains. Melanin is produced by cells in the lowest layer of the epidermis. It protects against the harmful, ultraviolet rays in sunlight, which can damage skin cells and the tissues underneath. Sensible exposure to the sun increases melanin production and darkens the skin. Sudden exposure of pale skin to strong sunlight can produce sunburn. People who live in, or whose ancestors lived in, hot countries produce more protective melanin and have darker skins.

Eyes and seeing

Vision is the body's dominant sense. It provides an enormous amount of information about our surroundings during every waking moment. The organs of vision are the eyes, which contain more than 70 percent of the body's sensory receptors in the form of light-detecting cells. Our eyes move automatically, adjust to changing light conditions, and focus light from objects near or far away. This focused light is converted by the light detectors into electrical signals that travel to the brain. Here those signals are changed into colored, three-dimensional images.

CROSS-EYED
This Arabic drawing, nearly 1,000 years old, shows the optic nerves crossing. Half of the nerve fibers from the right eye pass to the left side of the brain, where they are processed, and vice versa.

Medial rectus turns the eye inward toward the nose

Superior rectus moves the eye upward

Superior oblique muscle rotates the eye downward and outward, away from the nose

OUTER LAYERS
The wall of the eyeball is a three-layered sandwich. Outermost is the tough sclera, visible at the front as the white of the eye, except where the clear cornea allows light in. In the middle is the choroid, which is filled with blood vessels that supply the other two layers. The innermost layer is the light-detecting retina. Its millions of light detecting cells send image information to the brain.

Lateral rectus moves the eye outward

Inferior oblique rotates the eye upward and outward

Inferior rectus moves the eye downward

MOVING THE EYE
Eyeballs swivel in their sockets to follow moving objects. They also make tiny, jumping movements when scanning a face or the words on this page. The six slim muscles that produce all these movements are attached to the sclera at one end and the skull at the other. The muscles work as a team to move the eye in all directions.

Suspensory ligament

Fovea

Pupil is the hole in the center of the iris

EYELIDS AND TEARS
Soft, flexible eyelids protect the eyes and wash them with tears at each blink. Tears are produced by a lacrimal (tear) gland behind each upper eyelid, and flow out along tiny ducts (tubes) to be smeared over the eye's surface with each blink. Tears keep the eye moist and wash away dust and other irritants. People cry—produce excess tears—when they are sad, happy, or in pain. Used tear fluid drains away through two tiny holes in the eyelids near the nose, and along two tear ducts into the nose. That's why a good cry produces a runny nose, too.

Cornea

Lens

Iris

Ciliary muscles

Sclera

EYES FORWARD

Only one-sixth of an eyeball, including the pupil and iris, can be seen from the outside. The rest of each eyeball sits protected within a deep bowl of skull bone called the eye socket. Eyebrows, eyelids, and eyelashes protect the front of the eye by shading it from dust, sweat, and excessive light. The color of the iris depends on the amount of the brown pigment melanin present. Brown eyes have the most melanin.

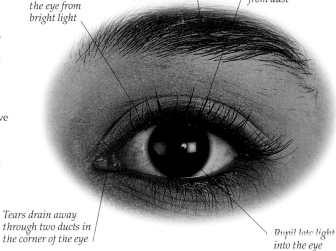

Eyebrows direct sweat away from the eye

Eyelids protect the eye from bright light

Eyelashes protect the eye from dust

Tears drain away through two ducts in the corner of the eye

Pupil lets light into the eye

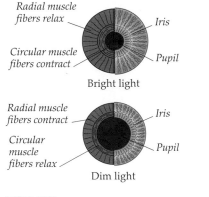

Radial muscle fibers relax

Circular muscle fibers contract

Iris

Pupil

Bright light

Radial muscle fibers contract

Circular muscle fibers relax

Iris

Pupil

Dim light

PUPIL SIZE

Muscle fibers (red) in the iris (blue) automatically adjust the size of the pupil. To prevent dazzling in bright light, circular fibers contract to make the pupil smaller. In dim conditions, to let in more light, radial fibers arranged like the spokes of a wheel contract to make the pupil larger.

Vitreous humor within the body of the eyeball

Blind spot is the area that lacks rods and cones

Optic nerve carries nerve signals from the retina to the brain

FORMING AN IMAGE

When we look at an object, light rays reflected from that object shine through and are partly focused, or bent, by the cornea. The light then passes through the pupil to the lens. Ciliary muscles adjust the lens's shape, and further focus the rays, which projects a sharp upside-down image onto the retina. The retina sends nerve signals along the optic nerve to the brain, which then turns the image the right way up.

Partial focus by the cornea

Fine-tune focus by the lens

Upside-down image formed at the back of the retina

Light rays from the object transmitted to the eye

Lens shape is adjusted by the ciliary muscles

Optic nerve

THE SEEING CELLS

This SEM reveals two kinds of light-detecting cells in the retina. The rods (green) see only in shades of gray, but they respond well in dim light. The cones (blue) are mainly in the fovea at the back of the retina and see details and colors, but work well only in bright light. Each eye has about 120 million rods and 6 or 7 million cones.

Retina

Choroid

INSIDE THE EYE

Behind the cornea, the colored iris controls the amount of light entering the eye through the pupil. The suspensory ligament holds the clear, curved lens in place, and the space behind it is filled with jellylike vitreous humor, which helps shape the eyeball. The most detailed images are produced where light falls on the fovea, the section of retina that contains only cones (see above right).

EYE ADVANCES

German scientist Hermann von Helmholtz (1821–94) made many advances in mathematics and physics, and wrote about the human body, including the *Handbook of Physiological Optics* (1856–67). He also helped to invent the ophthalmoscope. Doctors use this light-and-lens device for close-up examinations of the eye's interior.

Ears and hearing

AFTER SIGHT, HEARING IS THE SENSE that provides the brain with most information about the outside world. It enables humans to figure out the source, direction, and nature of sounds, and to communicate with each other. The ears also play an important part in the sense of balance. Ears work by detecting invisible waves of pressure, called sound waves, which travel through the air from a vibrating sound source. The ears turn these waves into nerve signals, which the brain interprets as sounds. Human ears can hear a fairly wide range of sounds. These vary in volume from the delicate notes of a flute to the ear-splitting chords of an electric guitar. Sounds also range in pitch from the growling of a dog to the high trills of bird song. In the ancient world, ears and hearing did not figure greatly in the works of scientists and physicians. Serious scientific study of hearing only began in the 1500s.

THE MIND'S EAR
The German composer and pianist, Ludwig van Beethoven (1770–1827), started to go deaf in his late twenties. He resolved to overcome his hearing handicap and continued to compose masterpieces by imagining the notes in his head.

EAR PIONEER
The Examination of the Organ of Hearing, published in 1562, was probably the first major work devoted to ears. Its author was the Italian Bartolomeo Eustachio (c. 1520–74), a professor of anatomy in Rome. His name lives on in the Eustachian tube that he discovered, which connects the middle ear to the back of the throat.

THE EARDRUM
The eardrum is a taut, delicate membrane, like the stretched skin on a drum, that vibrates when sound waves enter the ear. It separates the outer ear from the middle ear. Doctors can examine the eardrum by placing a medical instrument called an otoscope into the outer ear canal. Through the eardrum, there is a hazy view of the hammer, the first of three ear ossicles (see opposite).

Hammer is attached behind the eardrum

WHY EARS POP
The Eustachian tube allows air from the throat into the middle ear. This ensures equal air pressure on either side of the eardrum. When the eardrum vibrates freely, a person can hear clearly. Sudden changes in outside air pressure—as experienced on board a plane at take off or landing—can impair hearing because the eardrum cannot vibrate normally. Yawning or swallowing opens the Eustachian tube and causes the ears to pop, as air moves into the middle ear to restore equal pressures.

Eustachian (auditory) tube

18th-century drawing of the ear

Temporal bone of the skull

Scalp muscle

Cartilage supporting the pinna

Outer ear canal

INSIDE THE EAR
Most of the ear is concealed inside the skull's temporal bone. It has three main parts. The outer ear consists of the pinna (ear flap) that directs sound waves into the ear canal. The air-filled middle ear contains the eardrum and three tiny bones, the ossicles, which convert the sound waves into mechanical movement. The fluid-filled inner ear is made up of the semicircular canals, the vestibule, and the snail-shaped cochlea—the organ that converts sound into nerve signals.

Ear lobe of the pinna (ear flap)

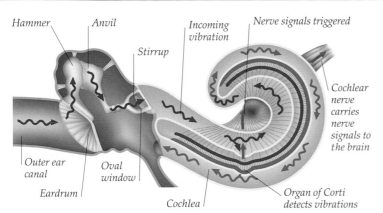

Hammer

Anvil

Stirrup

Incoming
vibration

Nerve signals triggered

Cochlear
nerve
carries
nerve
signals to
the brain

Outer ear
canal

Oval
window

Eardrum

Cochlea

Organ of Corti
detects vibrations

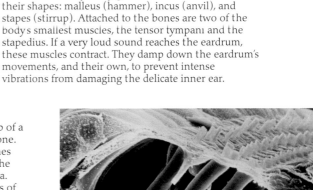

Incus (anvil)

Stapedius
muscle

Tensor
tympani
muscle

Stapes
(stirrup)

Malleus (hammer)

SMALLEST BONES
The ossicles (ear bones)
are tiny. The malleus
(hammer) is shown here
actual size. It is just over
¼ in (8 mm) long, almost
twice the size of the
stapes (stirrup).

HEARING

The ear collects sound waves, which funnel into the ear canal and
strike the eardrum, making it vibrate. This causes the three ossicles
(ear bones), linked by miniature joints, to move back and forth. The
innermost ossicle, the stirrup, pushes and pulls the flexible oval
window like a piston. This sets up vibrations in the fluid filling the
cochlea. The central tube of the cochlea contains the sound-detecting
organ of Corti, which turns the vibrations into nerve signals. These
pass along the cochlear nerve to the hearing area of the brain.

OSSICLES

The ossicles spanning the middle ear are the smallest
bones in the body. They get their Latin names from
their shapes: malleus (hammer), incus (anvil), and
stapes (stirrup). Attached to the bones are two of the
body's smallest muscles, the tensor tympani and the
stapedius. If a very loud sound reaches the eardrum,
these muscles contract. They damp down the eardrum's
movements, and their own, to prevent intense
vibrations from damaging the delicate inner ear.

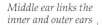

Middle ear links the
inner and outer ears

Semicircular
canals

THE INNER EAR

The innermost part of the ear is made up of a
maze of channels inside the temporal bone.
These channels are lined with membranes
and filled with fluid. One branch of the
inner ear leads to the coiled cochlea.
The vestibule contains two organs of
balance, the utricle and saccule. It
also houses the oval window, the
membrane through which sound
vibrations pass from middle to
inner ears. Another balance
organ, the semicircular canals,
lies above the vestibule.

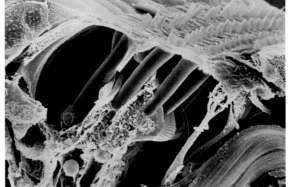

Vestibular nerve
carries signals from
the balance organs
to the brain

Cochlea

Cochlear nerve
carries signals from
the cochlea to the brain

Vestibule contains
the utricle and
saccule balance
organs

ORGAN OF CORTI

The organ of Corti consists of rows of hair cells (red), each
topped by a V-shaped tuft of hairs (yellow). When sound
vibrations pass through the cochlea's fluid, the hair cells
move up and down. This squashes the hairs, causing the
hair cells to send signals to the brain.

Eardrum
divides the
outer ear
from the
middle ear

Oval
window

Ossicles (ear bones)
link the eardrum to
the oval window

Eustachian
(auditory) tube

BALANCING ACT

The inner ear contains
the organs that help
the body maintain
balance. The three
semicircular canals
detect rotation of the
head in any direction.
The utricle and saccule
identify the position
of the head. They also
detect acceleration, as
experienced when
traveling up or down
in an elevator. These
balance organs
constantly update the
brain, so that it can
keep the body upright.

Smell and taste

THE SENSES OF SMELL and taste are closely linked because they both detect chemicals. Taste receptors on the tongue detect substances in drink and in chewed food. Olfactory (smell) receptors in the nasal cavity pick up odor molecules in air. Together, the senses of smell and taste enable us to enjoy the flavors of food and drink. Smell is 10,000 times more sensitive than taste, so if the nose is blocked, food loses its flavor. The two senses also help to protect us from harm. They can identify smells such as smoke that may indicate danger, or the bitter tastes of spoiled or poisonous food.

BAD AIR
For centuries, physicians believed that diseases were caused and spread by foul-smelling air. This 14th-century physician holds a pomander, or a container of aromatic herbs, to his nose to mask bad smells and protect him from catching his patient's illness.

Left cerebral hemisphere of the brain

Skull bone

Olfactory bulb carries the smell signals to the front of the brain

Branching olfactory nerves connect to the olfactory bulb

Nasal conchae (shelves of bone covered in nasal lining) keep the air inside the nose moist

Nasal cavity connects the nostrils to the throat

Mouth cavity

Tongue surface is covered with papillae, bearing taste buds

Chorda tympani branch of the facial nerve carries taste signals from the front two-thirds of the tongue

One of the muscles that move the tongue

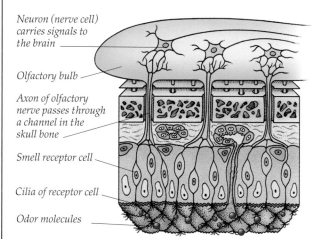

Neuron (nerve cell) carries signals to the brain

Olfactory bulb

Axon of olfactory nerve passes through a channel in the skull bone

Smell receptor cell

Cilia of receptor cell

Odor molecules

INSIDE THE NOSE
This cross-section gives a close-up view of the roof of the nasal cavity. Its lining (pink) contains thousands of smell receptor cells that detect odor molecules in the air. One end of each receptor ends in a cluster of hairlike cilia that project into the watery mucus of the nasal lining. The other end connects through the axons (nerve fibers) of the olfactory nerve to the olfactory bulb and the brain.

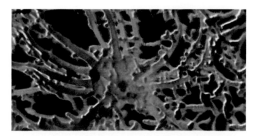

ODOR DETECTORS
This SEM shows the cilia at the tip of a receptor cell. Odor molecules dissolve in mucus and bind to the cilia, causing the receptor cells to send signals to the brain. Olfactory receptors can distinguish between 10,000 different smells.

SMELL AND TASTE PATHWAYS
This cross-section through the head shows the pathways taken by nerve signals from smell receptors high in the nasal cavity, and from taste buds in the tongue. In the nasal cavity, branches of the olfactory nerve send signals to the olfactory bulb, which carries the signals to areas at the front of the brain that identify smells. Taste signals from the front and back of the tongue travel along separate nerves to the brain stem's medulla oblongata. From here they are sent to the gustatory (taste) area of the brain where tastes are recognized.

Vallate papillae detect bitter tastes

Filiform papillae detect temperature and texture

Vagus nerve carries signals from taste buds in the throat

Glossopharyngeal nerve carries taste signals from the back of the tongue

Lingual nerve carries touch signals from the front of the tongue

Facial nerve carries taste signals from the front of the tongue

Fungiform papillae detect four different tastes

TASTE ORGAN
The muscular tongue mixes and tastes food during chewing. Its upper surface is covered with pimple-like papillae of different types. These make the tongue sensitive to taste and also to touch and temperature. The tongue's many nerves carry different types of sensory information to different parts of the brain.

Gustatory (taste) area on the left side of the brain

Pons (part of the brain stem) carries signals from the medulla oblongata to the brain

Medulla oblongata (part of the brain stem) receives signals from the facial and glossopharyngeal nerves

Spinal cord

Glossopharyngeal nerve carries taste signals from the rear one-third of the tongue

Throat

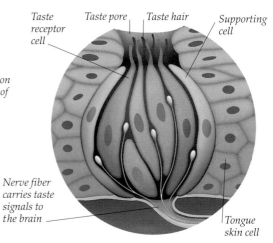

Taste receptor cell

Taste pore

Taste hair

Supporting cell

Nerve fiber carries taste signals to the brain

Tongue skin cell

TASTE BUDS
There are around 10,000 taste buds on the tongue. These taste sensors are located in the side and top of certain papillae. Taste molecules dissolve in saliva during chewing and pass into a taste bud through a pore. Here the hairs at the top of the taste receptor cells detect one of five tastes—sweet, sour, salty, bitter, or umami (savory).

PAPILLAE AND TASTE BUDS
This SEM shows two types of papillae at the front end of the tongue. The larger fungiform (mushroom-shaped) papillae contain taste buds. Spiky filiform papillae have no taste buds, but they give the tongue its rough surface that grips food during chewing. Filiform papillae also contain receptors that detect the texture and temperature of food.

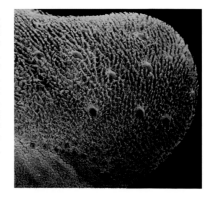

Chemical messengers

THE BODY HAS A SECOND CONTROL system that works alongside the brain and nerve network. The endocrine system is a collection of glands that release chemical messengers, called hormones, into the bloodstream. Hormones control body processes, such as growth and reproduction, by targeting specific body cells and altering their chemical activities. The nervous system uses electrical signals and works rapidly. The endocrine system works more slowly and has longer-lasting effects. The most important endocrine gland, the pituitary, controls several other endocrine glands. In turn, the pituitary gland is controlled by the hypothalamus, the part of the brain that links the two control systems.

Hypothalamus

Nerve cells in the front of the hypothalamus produce the hormones oxytocin and ADH

Pituitary stalk connects the hypothalamus to the pituitary gland

Blood vessels carry regulating hormones from the hypothalamus to the front of the pituitary gland

Front lobe of the pituitary gland is stimulated to release its hormones by regulating hormones from the hypothalamus

Vein carries hormones to the body

Pituitary gland
Thyroid gland
Thymus gland
Adrenal glands on top of the kidneys
Pancreas
Ovary in female
Testis in male

ENDOCRINE SYSTEM
The glands that make up the endocrine system lie inside the head and torso. Some endocrine glands, such as the thyroid, are organs in their own right. Other glands are embedded in an organ that also has other functions. The hormone-producing islet cells, for example, are part of the pancreas.

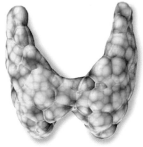

THYROID GLAND
Located in the neck, the butterfly-shaped thyroid gland makes two main hormones. Thyroxine targets most body cells and increases their metabolic (chemical-processing) rate to stimulate body growth and development. Calcitonin triggers the uptake of bone-building calcium from the blood into bones.

FIGHT OR FLIGHT
The hormone epinephrine (also called adrenaline) prepares the body for action in the face of danger. It acts rapidly by boosting heart and breathing rates and diverting blood and extra glucose (sugar) to the muscles. This readies the body to fight danger or flee from it.

Right kidney
Adrenal gland

ADRENAL GLANDS
An adrenal gland sits on top of each kidney. Its outer part, the cortex, makes several hormones called corticosteroids. Their roles include regulating the levels of water and salts in the bloodstream, speeding up the body's metabolism (chemical processes), and coping with stress. The inner part of the kidney, called the medulla, is controlled by the nervous system. It releases adrenaline, which prepares the body to deal with threats (see left).

HYPOTHALAMUS

Situated at the center of the base of the brain, the hypothalamus controls a range of body activities. Some of this control is enforced through the pituitary gland. Neurons (nerve cells) in the rear of the hypothalamus produce regulating hormones that travel in the bloodstream to the front lobe of the pituitary. Here they stimulate the release of pituitary hormones. Neurons in the front of the hypothalamus make two hormones that pass down the axons (nerve fibers) to the rear lobe of the pituitary gland where they are stored before release.

Nerve cells in the rear of the hypothalamus release regulating hormones into the blood vessels supplying the front lobe

PANCREAS

The pancreas has two roles. Most of its tissues consist of gland cells, which make digestive enzymes for release along ducts into the small intestine (pp. 54–55). The pancreas also has endocrine tissues, which release the hormones insulin and glucagon directly into the bloodstream. These two hormones maintain steady levels of glucose—the sugar removed from food to fuel the body—in the blood.

Nerve fibers carry oxytocin and ADH from the hypothalamus to the rear lobe of the pituitary gland

Artery carries fresh blood into the pituitary

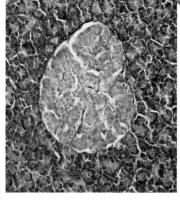

PANCREATIC ISLETS

This microscopic image shows the tissue inside the pancreas. It is dotted with more than one million clusters of cells called islets of Langerhans (center). They are named after the German physician Paul Langerhans (1847–88), who first saw them under a microscope in 1869. In the 1890s, scientists discovered that the islet cells released secretions, which were later called hormones.

Sir Frederick Banting
(1891–1941)

Charles Best
(1899–1978)

THE INSULIN STORY

A lack of the hormone insulin in the body causes a serious condition called diabetes, where blood glucose levels soar. In 1922, Canadian Frederick Banting and American Charles Best successfully extracted insulin so that it could be used to treat and control this potentially fatal disorder. Banting received a Nobel Prize in 1923, but he shared his prize money with Best.

Rear lobe of the pituitary gland stores and releases ADH and oxytocin

PITUITARY GLAND

The pea-sized pituitary gland is attached to the base of the brain and has completely separate front and rear lobes, or parts. Front lobe cells make and release six hormones that affect growth, reproduction, and metabolism, usually by stimulating another endocrine gland to release hormones. The rear lobe stores and releases antidiuretic hormone (ADH), which controls the water content of urine, and oxytocin, which makes the uterus contract during labor.

THYMUS GLAND

Located under the breastbone, the thymus gland is large during childhood but shrinks in adult life. During a child's early years, it produces two hormones that ensure the normal development of white blood cells called T cells, or T lymphocytes (p. 45). These cells play a vital part in fighting disease by identifying and destroying disease-causing organisms, such as bacteria. This SEM shows undeveloped T lymphocytes (yellow) inside the thymus gland.

The heart

ORGAN STORAGE
When the ancient Egyptians prepared mummies, they removed most body organs and stored them in jars such as these. Only the heart, believed to be the seat of the soul, was left in place, ready for the afterlife.

THE ANCIENT GREEKS BELIEVED that the heart was the seat of love and intelligence. Thanks to discoveries made in the 17th century, we know that the heart is an extraordinarily reliable, muscular pump, and that the brain is home to love and emotions. Those discoveries also revealed that the human heart has separate right and left sides. Each side has two linked chambers, or compartments—an upper, thin-walled atrium with a much larger, thick-walled ventricle below. Each ventricle pumps blood along a different circulatory route. In the pulmonary (lung) circulation, the right ventricle pumps oxygen-poor blood to the lungs to pick up oxygen and then back to the left atrium. In the systemic (body) circulation, the left ventricle pumps oxygen-rich blood around the body and back to the right atrium. The heart wall consists mainly of cardiac muscle, a type of muscle that never tires. Over an average lifetime, a heart will beat some 2.5 billion times without stopping for a rest.

THE RIGHT CONNECTIONS
Italian anatomist and botanist Andrea Cesalpino (1519–1603) produced a remarkably accurate description of how the heart connects to the main blood vessels and the lungs. However, he incorrectly stated that blood flows out of the heart along all vessels, the veins as well as the arteries.

Right coronary artery

Aorta

Left coronary artery

Coronary vein

Coronary sinus (main coronary vein)

Small connecting blood vessels

Main branch of the left coronary artery

CORONARY CIRCULATION
The heart's muscular wall does not obtain oxygen or food from the blood that gushes through the atria and ventricles. Instead it has its own blood supply called the coronary circulation, which delivers oxygen to keep the heart beating. Left and right coronary arteries stem from the aorta and branch out to carry oxygen-rich blood to all parts of the heart wall. Oxygen-poor blood is collected by coronary veins that drain into the coronary sinus. This large vein at the back of the heart empties blood into the right atrium to start its passage through the heart again.

Valve open

Valve closed

Blood flows away from the heart

Blood pushes through the open valve as the heart contracts

Blood flows back and shuts the valve as the heart relaxes

Blood is pumped out of the heart

VALVES AT WORK
Valves ensure an efficient, one-way flow of blood. The pulmonary and aortic valves at the two exits from the heart have pocket-shaped flaps of tissue. When the heart contracts, blood pushes its way out, flattening the pockets against the wall. When the heart relaxes, blood tries to flow back, opening out the pockets to close off the valve. The bicuspid and tricuspid valves between the heart chambers work in a similar way.

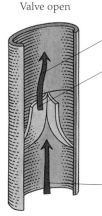

HEART RATE
In a resting body, the average adult heart beats 60–80 times, pumping up to 12½ pints (6 liters) of blood every minute. Each beat creates a pressure surge through the body's network of arteries. This surge can be felt in the radial artery in the wrist, and is called the pulse. During activity, the muscles need more oxygen and nutrients. The heart beats faster and harder, as much as 150 times a minute, to circulate up to 9 gallons (35 liters) of blood in the fittest individuals.

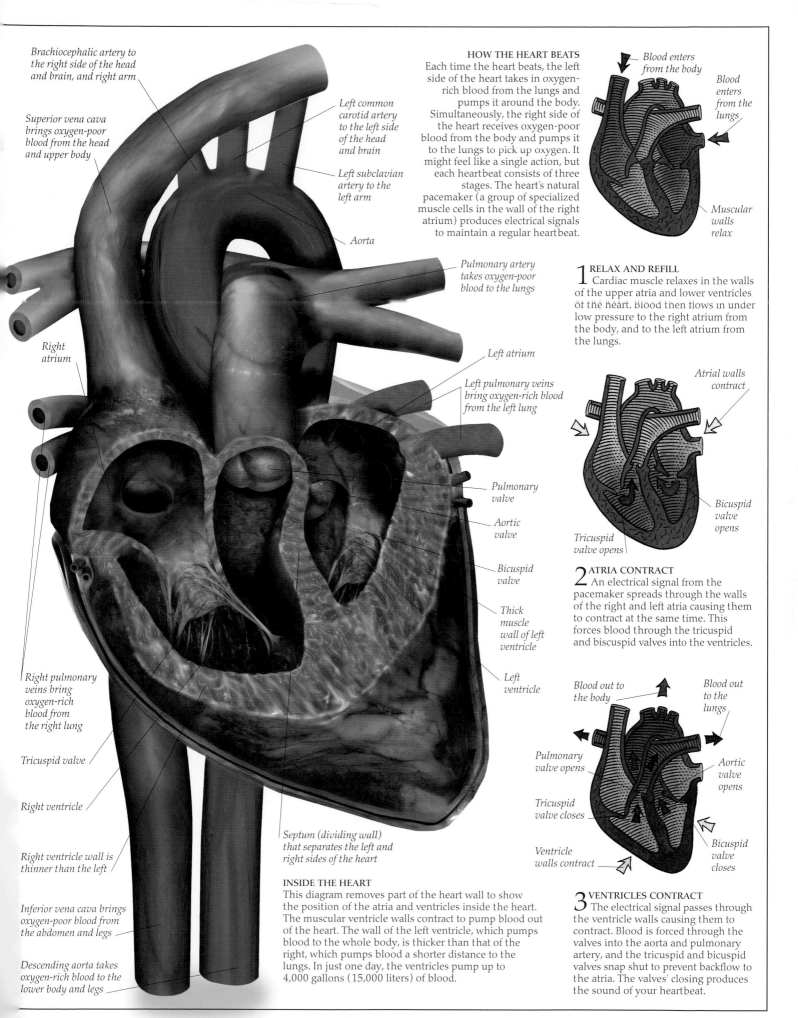

Brachiocephalic artery to the right side of the head and brain, and right arm

Superior vena cava brings oxygen-poor blood from the head and upper body

Right atrium

Right pulmonary veins bring oxygen-rich blood from the right lung

Tricuspid valve

Right ventricle

Right ventricle wall is thinner than the left

Inferior vena cava brings oxygen-poor blood from the abdomen and legs

Descending aorta takes oxygen-rich blood to the lower body and legs

Left common carotid artery to the left side of the head and brain

Left subclavian artery to the left arm

Aorta

Pulmonary artery takes oxygen-poor blood to the lungs

Left atrium

Left pulmonary veins bring oxygen-rich blood from the left lung

Pulmonary valve

Aortic valve

Bicuspid valve

Thick muscle wall of left ventricle

Left ventricle

Septum (dividing wall) that separates the left and right sides of the heart

INSIDE THE HEART
This diagram removes part of the heart wall to show the position of the atria and ventricles inside the heart. The muscular ventricle walls contract to pump blood out of the heart. The wall of the left ventricle, which pumps blood to the whole body, is thicker than that of the right, which pumps blood a shorter distance to the lungs. In just one day, the ventricles pump up to 4,000 gallons (15,000 liters) of blood.

HOW THE HEART BEATS
Each time the heart beats, the left side of the heart takes in oxygen-rich blood from the lungs and pumps it around the body. Simultaneously, the right side of the heart receives oxygen-poor blood from the body and pumps it to the lungs to pick up oxygen. It might feel like a single action, but each heartbeat consists of three stages. The heart's natural pacemaker (a group of specialized muscle cells in the wall of the right atrium) produces electrical signals to maintain a regular heartbeat.

Blood enters from the body

Blood enters from the lungs

Muscular walls relax

1 RELAX AND REFILL
Cardiac muscle relaxes in the walls of the upper atria and lower ventricles of the heart. Blood then flows in under low pressure to the right atrium from the body, and to the left atrium from the lungs.

Atrial walls contract

Bicuspid valve opens

Tricuspid valve opens

2 ATRIA CONTRACT
An electrical signal from the pacemaker spreads through the walls of the right and left atria causing them to contract at the same time. This forces blood through the tricuspid and biscuspid valves into the ventricles.

Blood out to the body

Blood out to the lungs

Pulmonary valve opens

Aortic valve opens

Tricuspid valve closes

Bicuspid valve closes

Ventricle walls contract

3 VENTRICLES CONTRACT
The electrical signal passes through the ventricle walls causing them to contract. Blood is forced through the valves into the aorta and pulmonary artery, and the tricuspid and bicuspid valves snap shut to prevent backflow to the atria. The valves' closing produces the sound of your heartbeat.

In circulation

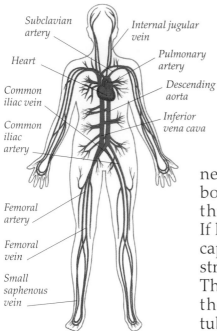

CIRCULATORY SYSTEM
This simplified view of the circulatory system shows the major blood vessels that extend out from the heart to all parts of the body. Arteries carry oxygen-rich blood from the heart to body tissues, and veins return oxygen-poor blood to the heart from the tissues. Capillaries, too small to be seen here, carry blood through the tissues and connect arteries to veins.

Subclavian artery
Internal jugular vein
Heart
Pulmonary artery
Common iliac vein
Descending aorta
Common iliac artery
Inferior vena cava
Femoral artery
Femoral vein
Small saphenous vein

Each of the body's trillions of cells demands a constant supply of oxygen, nutrients, and other essentials, and the constant removal of wastes. The body's circulatory system meets these needs. The heart pumps blood around the body, delivering essentials to cells through a vast network of blood vessels. If laid end to end, this network of capillaries, arteries, and veins would stretch over 62,000 miles (100,000 km). The capillaries make up 98 percent of the body's blood vessels. These tiny tubes, barely wider than the blood cells that flow through them, pass by almost every body cell. A second transportation system, called the lymphatic system, drains excess fluid from the tissues. The circulatory and lymphatic systems both play key parts in defending the body against disease.

External iliac artery
External iliac vein
Pelvis (hip bone)
Femoral vein carries blood from the thigh
Branch of femoral artery supplies blood to the thigh
Great saphenous vein carries blood from the foot and leg

William Harvey

ROUND AND ROUND
Until the 17th century, it was believed that blood flowed backward and forward inside arteries and veins. English physician William Harvey (1578–1657) conducted experiments that showed how the heart pumped blood around the body in one direction. Harvey, shown here explaining this theory to King Charles I, published his findings in 1628 in *On the Movement of the Heart and Blood*.

BLOOD VESSELS OF THE LEG
This model of the left leg shows how the blood vessels of the circulatory system divide and branch into smaller and smaller vessels. For example, the large external iliac artery carries oxygen-rich blood from the heart to the leg. Here it divides into branches that then subdivide to form the microscopic capillaries that deliver oxygen and nutrients to cells, and remove their waste products. The capillaries then rejoin, forming larger vessels that connect into the network of major veins. The external iliac vein is the main vessel carrying oxygen-poor blood from the leg back toward the heart.

Small saphenous vein carries blood from the foot and lower leg

Small posterior tibial arteries supply blood to the foot and lower leg

VESSEL INVESTIGATOR
Swiss-born Albrecht von Haller (1708–77) was a botanist, anatomist, and poet who wrote a book on physiology. He investigated how the muscle layer in the wall of smaller arteries could contract or relax to vary the amount of blood flowing to a particular body part.

VEIN VALVES
Harvey based his theory of blood circulation on careful study, rather than following tradition. His approach marked the beginning of scientific medicine. Harvey's illustrations show how the blood in veins always flows toward the heart. Valves, here marked by letters, prevent it from seeping backward.

BLOOD VESSELS

An artery has thick layers of muscle and elastic tissue in its walls to withstand blood at high pressure direct from the heart. It can expand and shrink as blood surges through it with every heartbeat. Veins carry blood returning from capillaries at low pressure, so their wall layers are thinner and less muscular. Capillary walls are just one cell thick, allowing food and oxygen to pass from blood into the surrounding tissues.

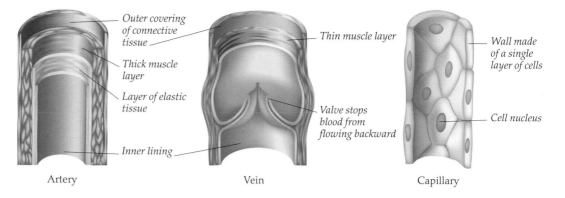

Outer covering of connective tissue

Thick muscle layer

Layer of elastic tissue

Inner lining

Thin muscle layer

Valve stops blood from flowing backward

Wall made of a single layer of cells

Cell nucleus

Artery   Vein   Capillary

Fighting infection

Every day, the body is exposed to pathogens—microscopic organisms, such as bacteria and viruses, that cause disease if they manage to invade the body's tissues and bloodstream. The body fights infections with white blood cells in the circulatory and lymphatic systems. Together, these form the body's immune, or defense, system. Some white blood cells patrol the body and search for invading organisms to destroy. Others, particularly those found in the lymph nodes, launch attacks against specific pathogens and retain a memory of them, in case the same pathogens return to infect the body again.

IMMUNE SYSTEM

The macrophages and lymphocytes—white blood cells also called T and B cells—of the immune system respond to the invasion of pathogens by detecting and destroying them. If the same pathogen returns, the immune system's response is even faster.

Macrophage

Shigella bacterium

1 CAPTURING A PATHOGEN
Macrophages are white blood cells that hunt for pathogens in the body's tissues. This one has tracked down and captured a disease-causing bacterium called *Shigella*. The macrophage reaches out to swallow the bacterium, before digesting it.

Lymph vessels drain lymph from the tissues

Thymus gland processes lymphocytes

Lymph empties into the blood at the subclavian artery

Thoracic duct

Lymph nodes clustered around the groin

Spleen produces large numbers of lymphocytes

2 RECOGNIZING ANTIGENS
The macrophage displays the antigens, or remains of the bacterium, on its surface. These are recognized by a lymphocyte called a helper T cell, which is now activated.

Antigens (remains of the destroyed bacterium)

Antibodies attach themselves to a Shigella bacterium

5 DISABLING THE PATHOGEN
Antibodies tag the *Shigella* bacterium by binding to the antigens on its surface. This disables the bacterium and marks it for destruction by macrophages or other white blood cells.

Antibody

Helper T cell

B cell

Plasma cell

LYMPHATIC SYSTEM

This network of vessels drains excess fluid from the body's tissues and returns it to the bloodstream. The lymphatic system has no pump; instead the contractions of skeletal muscles push the fluid, called lymph, along the lymph vessels. As it flows, lymph passes through small swellings called lymph nodes. These contain masses of macrophages and lymphocytes, the white blood cells that detect and destroy pathogens.

3 SPURRED INTO ACTION
The activated helper T cell releases substances that switch on a B cell, which specifically targets *Shigella*. The B cell multiplies by dividing rapidly to produce identical plasma cells.

4 MAKING ANTIBODIES
Plasma cells release billions of antibody molecules into the blood and lymph. The antibodies track down any *Shigella* bacteria present in the body.

The blood

FEEDING ON BLEEDING
Leeches and vampire bats feed on the blood of other animals. This scene from the 1978 film *Nosferatu*, shows a mythical human vampire feeding on blood in order to gain immortality—a legend that turns up in tales of superstition around the world.

BLOOD TRANSFUSIONS
This 17th-century illustration shows transfusing (transferring) blood from a donor—usually a healthy person, but here a dog—to a sick patient. Before the discovery of blood groups (see opposite) in the 20th century, many transfusions failed, killing the patient.

Red blood cell has no nucleus and a dimpled shape

AN AVERAGE ADULT HAS 9 PINTS (5 liters) of red, liquid tissue coursing around the body, pumped along blood vessels by the heart. Blood consists of a mixture of cell types floating in liquid plasma. For example, just a single drop of blood contains as many as 250 million red blood cells. These flow through the body's tissues, delivering essential oxygen to trillions of cells 24 hours a day. Blood also distributes heat to keep the body at a steady 98.6°F (37°C)—the ideal internal temperature for cell operations. When blood vessels are damaged and spring a leak, blood has its own repair system to prevent potentially dangerous blood loss. Blood also carries battalions of defense cells to fight off infections and protect the body from disease.

RED AND WHITE BLOOD CELLS
Each type of blood cell has a vital role to play in the body. Red blood cells, by far the most numerous, transport oxygen to body cells. White blood cells, including neutrophils and lymphocytes, are involved in defending the body against pathogens, or disease-causing germs. Neutrophils travel to sites of infection, track down pathogens such as disease-causing bacteria, and then eat them. Lymphocytes form part of the immune system (p. 45) that targets and destroys specific germs. Platelets help to seal wounds by forming blood clots.

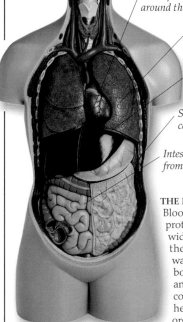

Heart pumps blood around the body

Lungs transfer oxygen and carbon dioxide to and from the blood

Liver controls the concentration of many chemicals in the blood

Spleen removes old, worn-out red blood cells, and helps to recycle their iron

Intestines transfer digested nutrients from food into the blood

THE ROLES OF BLOOD
Blood has three main roles—transportation, protection, and regulation. First, it transports a wide range of substances, including oxygen from the lungs, nutrients from the intestines, and waste products from cells. Second, it protects the body by carrying defensive white blood cells, and by forming blood clots. Third, it regulates or controls body temperature by distributing heat produced by the liver, muscles, and other organs around the body.

Neutrophil has a nucleus consisting of many lobes

Plasma makes up 55% of blood

White blood cells and platelets make up 1% of blood

Red blood cells make up 44% of blood

Settled blood

Oxygen-rich blood

Oxygen-poor blood

BLOOD COMPONENTS

Blood may appear to be a uniformly red liquid but, if allowed to settle, it separates into three parts, as shown above. The red and white blood cells float in a yellow liquid called plasma. Plasma is mainly water containing over 100 substances, including oxygen, nutrients, blood proteins, hormones, and wastes.

CHANGING COLOR

Blood takes its color from red blood cells. The depth of color changes as blood travels around the body. When red blood cells pick up oxygen in the lungs, blood turns bright red. Once they unload oxygen in the tissues, blood turns a darker shade of red.

BLOOD GROUPS

Austrian-born, American scientist Karl Landsteiner (1868–1943) discovered that people belonged to one of four blood groups. He named them A, B, AB, or O. During blood transfusions, a body often rejects blood of the wrong group. But today, transfusions are safe because doctors can match up blood types.

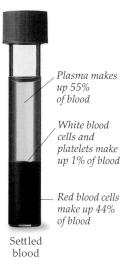

OXYGEN CARRIER

Hemoglobin is a protein that carries oxygen and gives red blood cells their color. This computer-generated image shows the structure of its molecules. Each molecule contains four iron atoms (yellow). The iron atoms bind oxygen in the lungs, where oxygen is abundant, and release it wherever oxygen is in short supply in the body. Inside a red blood cell, 250 million hemoglobin molecules can carry an astounding 1 billion molecules of oxygen.

Lymphocyte has a nucleus that fills most of the cell

Platelet is a cell fragment rather than a cell

FORMING BLOOD CLOTS

If a blood vessel is damaged, the blood automatically stops leakage and fights infection, as shown in this illustration of a skin wound. At the injury site, platelets stick together to form a temporary plug. They also release chemicals that convert a blood protein into threads of fibrin, which trap blood cells to form a jellylike clot. White blood cells, attracted to the wound, track down and destroy any invading bacteria. Eventually the clot dries out to form a scab. This protects the underlying tissues while they repair themselves.

A net of fibrin threads traps the blood cells

Scab eventually forms over wound

Invading germ such as bacteria

White blood cell destroys the germs inside the wound

Epidermis of the skin

Dermis

Platelet

Red blood cell

White blood cell moving to the wound

Blood vessel

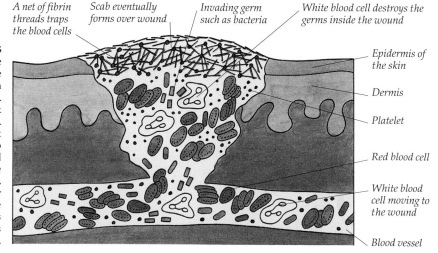

Breathing to live

THE BODY CAN SURVIVE WITHOUT FOOD or water for some time, but soon dies if breathing stops. Breathing brings fresh air containing oxygen into the lungs, and then expels stale air containing waste carbon dioxide. The respiratory system takes the oxygen from air to keep body cells alive. Since oxygen cannot be stored by the body, breathing needs to be a nonstop process. How breathing works was first explained in the 17th century by the physician John Mayow. He showed how the muscles of the chest and diaphragm made the lungs stretch and expand, drawing in air like bellows.

Nasal cavity (space) connects the nostrils to the throat

Three conchae (shelves of bone covered in nasal lining) keep the air inside the nose moist

Nostril contains nose hairs to filter out dirt

Mouth cavity

Esophagus

Tongue

Epiglottis

Vocal cords

Larynx (voice box)

Trachea (windpipe)

Nasal cavity

Intercostal muscles between the ribs

Trachea (windpipe)

Rib

Right lung

RESPIRATORY SYSTEM
The respiratory system carries air from outside the body through the airways to a pair of lungs. The airways consist of the nasal cavity, throat, larynx, and the trachea and its branches. The lungs are surrounded and protected by the ribs, which also play a part in breathing.

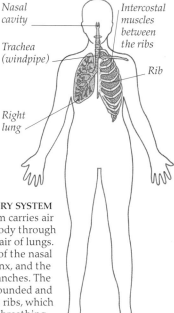

CONTROLLED BREATHING
The great jazz musicians Charlie Parker (left) and Miles Davis created wonderful music with the saxophone and trumpet, when performing together in the late 1940s. Musicians need excellent breath control to play wind instruments such as these. Precisely timed contractions of the diaphragm and rib muscles push bursts of air out of the mouth and into the instrument. Different notes can be played by varying the force and duration of the blowing.

UPPER AIRWAYS
The lungs have delicate tissues that are easily damaged by dirt particles, which must be removed in the upper airways after inhalation (breathing in). Nostril hairs filter out larger dirt particles. Sticky mucus covering the nasal lining traps dust and bacteria. Cold, dry air can also damage the delicate lung tissues, so the nasal cavity warms and moistens inhaled air, and also cleans it. The filtered air then passes into the larynx and on to the lungs.

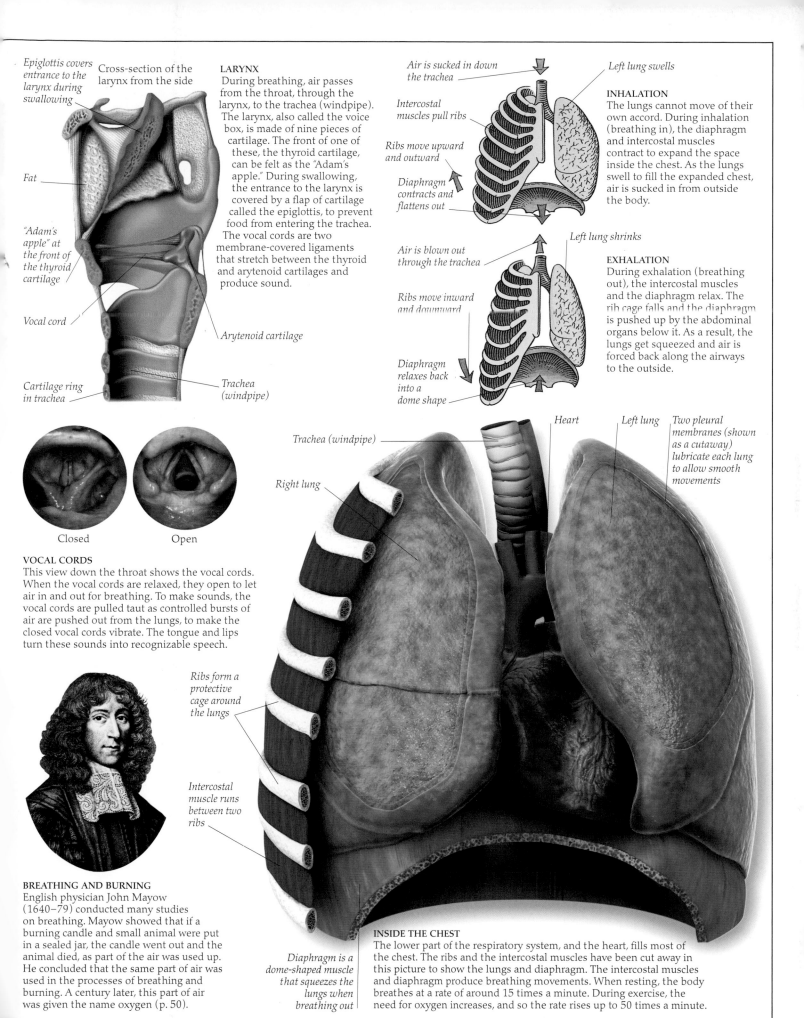

Epiglottis covers entrance to the larynx during swallowing

Cross-section of the larynx from the side

Fat

"Adam's apple" at the front of the thyroid cartilage

Vocal cord

Cartilage ring in trachea

Arytenoid cartilage

Trachea (windpipe)

LARYNX
During breathing, air passes from the throat, through the larynx, to the trachea (windpipe). The larynx, also called the voice box, is made of nine pieces of cartilage. The front of one of these, the thyroid cartilage, can be felt as the "Adam's apple." During swallowing, the entrance to the larynx is covered by a flap of cartilage called the epiglottis, to prevent food from entering the trachea. The vocal cords are two membrane-covered ligaments that stretch between the thyroid and arytenoid cartilages and produce sound.

Air is sucked in down the trachea

Left lung swells

Intercostal muscles pull ribs

Ribs move upward and outward

Diaphragm contracts and flattens out

INHALATION
The lungs cannot move of their own accord. During inhalation (breathing in), the diaphragm and intercostal muscles contract to expand the space inside the chest. As the lungs swell to fill the expanded chest, air is sucked in from outside the body.

Air is blown out through the trachea

Left lung shrinks

Ribs move inward and downward

Diaphragm relaxes back into a dome shape

EXHALATION
During exhalation (breathing out), the intercostal muscles and the diaphragm relax. The rib cage falls and the diaphragm is pushed up by the abdominal organs below it. As a result, the lungs get squeezed and air is forced back along the airways to the outside.

Closed

Open

VOCAL CORDS
This view down the throat shows the vocal cords. When the vocal cords are relaxed, they open to let air in and out for breathing. To make sounds, the vocal cords are pulled taut as controlled bursts of air are pushed out from the lungs, to make the closed vocal cords vibrate. The tongue and lips turn these sounds into recognizable speech.

Ribs form a protective cage around the lungs

Intercostal muscle runs between two ribs

BREATHING AND BURNING
English physician John Mayow (1640–79) conducted many studies on breathing. Mayow showed that if a burning candle and small animal were put in a sealed jar, the candle went out and the animal died, as part of the air was used up. He concluded that the same part of air was used in the processes of breathing and burning. A century later, this part of air was given the name oxygen (p. 50).

Trachea (windpipe)

Heart

Left lung

Two pleural membranes (shown as a cutaway) lubricate each lung to allow smooth movements

Right lung

Diaphragm is a dome-shaped muscle that squeezes the lungs when breathing out

INSIDE THE CHEST
The lower part of the respiratory system, and the heart, fills most of the chest. The ribs and the intercostal muscles have been cut away in this picture to show the lungs and diaphragm. The intercostal muscles and diaphragm produce breathing movements. When resting, the body breathes at a rate of around 15 times a minute. During exercise, the need for oxygen increases, and so the rate rises up to 50 times a minute.

Inside the lungs

THE LUNGS FEEL SPONGY because they are filled with millions of microscopic air sacs called alveoli. They appear pink because every alveolus is wrapped in a mesh of tiny blood vessels. Air is carried to the alveoli by a branching network of tubes stemming from the trachea. Alveoli remove oxygen from the air and pass it into the bloodstream, which delivers oxygen to every body cell. Here it is used to release energy from food in a chemical process known as cell respiration. The waste product is carbon dioxide, which is poisonous if it builds up, but it travels in the bloodstream to the alveoli where it is expelled. The swapping of oxygen and carbon dioxide in the lungs is called gas exchange. Two 18th-century scientists, Antoine Levoisier and Lazzaro Spallanzani, were pioneers in understanding the process.

ALL-OVER RESPIRATION
Italian scientist Lazzaro Spallanzani (1729–99) was professor of natural history at Pavia. Spallanzani was a contemporary of Lavoisier (see below left) and both viewed respiration as a process similar to burning. Spallanzani proposed that respiration took place not just in the lungs, but in every cell of the body. He also discovered that blood delivered oxygen to body tissues and carried away carbon dioxide.

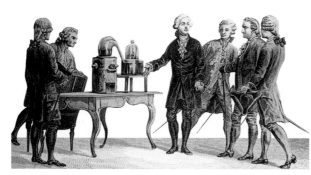

OXYGEN GETS ITS NAME
In the 1770s, French chemist Antoine Lavoisier (1743–94) showed that the wax of a candle burned using part of the air—a gas he called oxygen. He gave the name "fixed air" to the waste gas produced in burning (now called carbon dioxide). In 1783, Lavoisier suggested that animals live by burning food inside the lungs using the oxygen in air—a process he called respiration.

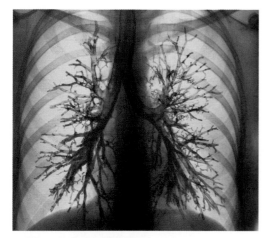

THE BRONCHIAL TREE
This colored chest X-ray shows the bronchial tree, a branching system of tubes that carries air throughout the lungs. The trachea divides into two bronchi, one to each lung. Each bronchus divides repeatedly, forming smaller bronchi, then bronchioles, and finally terminal bronchioles, narrower than a hair.

Upper lobe of the right lung

Branch of the right bronchus

Pulmonary artery is colored blue to show it carries oxygen-poor blood

Pulmonary vein is colored red to show it carries oxygen-rich blood

Small bronchus

Terminal (end) bronchioles are the narrowest bronchioles

Middle lobe of the right lung

Bottom lobe of the right lung

MICROBUBBLES

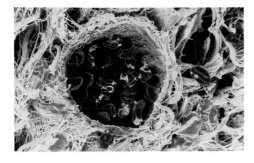

This SEM shows red blood cells in a tiny artery in lung tissue. Some have spilled out during preparation of the SEM. Surrounding the blood vessel are air-filled, bubblelike alveoli, each measuring less than 0.004 in (0.1 mm) across.

WHERE GAS EXCHANGE HAPPENS

Each terminal bronchiole, the narrowest branch of the bronchial tree, ends in grapelike bunches of alveoli. Together, the lungs contain over 300 million alveoli—with a combined surface area for gas exchange the size of a tennis-court. Around each alveolus is a network of blood capillaries that exchange gases with the alveolus.

Trachea (windpipe)

Aorta carries oxygen-rich blood from the heart

Pulmonary artery carries oxygen-poor blood to the lungs

Upper lobe of the left lung

Terminal bronchiole

Branch of the pulmonary vein

Branch of the pulmonary artery

Alveoli

Capillary network around the alveolus

Oxygen-poor blood rich in carbon dioxide

Carbon dioxide passes into the alveolus from the blood

Stale air leaves the alveolus by the terminal bronchiole

REFRESHED WITH OXYGEN

The walls of an alveolus and the capillary surrounding it are both incredibly thin. Sandwiched together they form a surface for gas exchange that is just 0.00004 in (0.001 mm) thick. Oxygen from the alveolus passes rapidly into the blood, turning its color from dark to bright red. Carbon dioxide moves in the opposite direction.

Oxygen passes from air in the alveolus into the blood

Blood rich in picked-up oxygen

Capillary

Fresh air enters the alveolus from the terminal bronchiole

LUNGS AND HEART

This cutaway illustration shows the air passages inside the right lung, which has three lobes. The left lung has two lobes and leaves space for the heart. This closeness between the heart and lungs means that blood travels only a short distance to pick up oxygen. Oxygen-poor blood flows from the right side of the heart along the pulmonary arteries to the lungs, where it is recharged with oxygen and discharges carbon dioxide. The oxygen-rich blood travels along the pulmonary veins to the heart's left side and is then pumped around the whole body.

Inferior vena cava delivers oxygen-poor blood to the heart

Heart (pp. 42–43)

Descending aorta carries oxygen-rich blood to the lower body

Lower lobe of the left lung

51

Eating

EATING FOOD IS ESSENTIAL FOR LIFE. Food supplies the nutrients—a mixture of carbohydrates, proteins, fats, and other substances—that give the body energy and provide the building blocks for growth and repair. To release these nutrients, food must be processed both mechanically and chemically in the digestive system. The mechanical process of eating and chewing breaks up food into smaller pieces. Saliva in the mouth begins the chemical process. It contains chemical digesters called enzymes that start breaking down complex foods into simple substances, which can be used by the body. Once food is swallowed, it continues on its digestive journey to the stomach.

Parotid salivary gland

Nasal cavity

Soft palate

Parotid duct

Pharynx (throat)

Tongue

Teeth

Sublingual duct

Sublingual salivary gland

Submandibular duct

Submandibular salivary gland

Epiglottis

Esophagus

Trachea (windpipe)

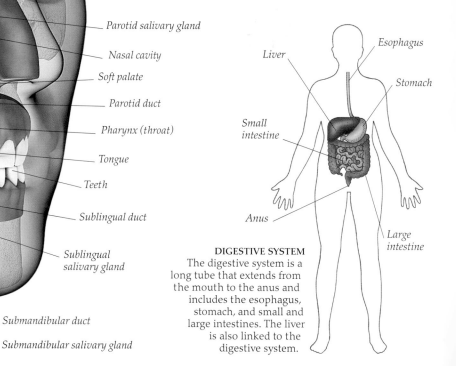

Liver

Esophagus

Stomach

Small intestine

Anus

Large intestine

DIGESTIVE SYSTEM
The digestive system is a long tube that extends from the mouth to the anus and includes the esophagus, stomach, and small and large intestines. The liver is also linked to the digestive system.

INSIDE THE MOUTH
When food arrives in the mouth, the lips, cheek muscles, and tongue guide it between the teeth. Taste buds on the tongue sample the food to see how delicious or unpleasant it is. As teeth cut and crush the food, three pairs of salivary glands squirt watery saliva along ducts into the mouth. Saliva contains mucus, which binds and lubricates food particles together. It also contains an enzyme that starts breaking down starch in the food.

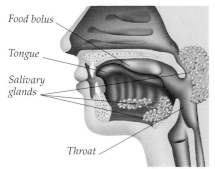

Food bolus
Tongue
Salivary glands
Throat

CHEWING A MOUTHFUL
As we chew, our teeth cut and crush food into small particles. Our tongue mixes the food with the sticky mucus in saliva to form a compact, slippery bolus, or ball of food. The tongue now presses the bolus against the roof of the mouth and pushes it backward into the throat.

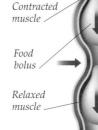

Soft palate lifted up
Food bolus enters the esophagus
Epiglottis covers entrance to the trachea

SWALLOWING
When the tongue pushes food into the throat, it triggers an automatic reflex action. The muscles in the wall of the throat contract, moving the bolus into the esophagus. The soft palate rises to prevent food from entering the nasal cavity.

Contracted muscle
Food bolus
Relaxed muscle

PERISTALSIS
Waves of muscle contractions, called peristalsis, squeeze the lubricated bolus down the esophagus to the stomach. Peristalsis also moves food through the intestines.

A BALANCED DIET
There are six main nutrients in food. Carbohydrates (starch and sugars) and fats supply energy. Proteins build and maintain the body. Vitamins and minerals ensure cells work properly, and bulky fiber helps the intestinal muscles work better. A balanced diet contains a mixture of all these nutrients in the right proportions. This meal includes starchy rice, fish and meat containing protein and fat, and vegetables rich in vitamins and minerals.

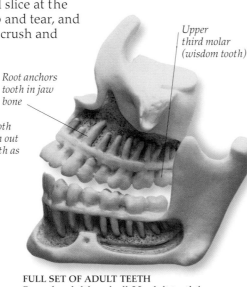

ENERGY RELEASE
British athlete Christina Ohuruogo wins a gold medal at the 2008 Olympic Games. Running, like any physical activity, requires the energy that comes from food. The digestive process converts food starches into sugars and fats into fatty acids. These are the fuels that release the energy for movement, when they are broken down inside muscle cells.

Teeth

We have two sets of teeth during our lifetime, which break up food in the mouth to make it easier to swallow and digest. Baby, or deciduous teeth, are replaced during childhood by a larger set of adult, or permanent, teeth. There are four types of adult teeth: chisel-like incisors that cut and slice at the front, pointed canines that grip and tear, and flat premolars and molars that crush and grind at the back.

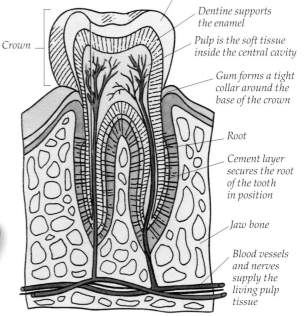

Crown
Enamel is the tooth's hard surface material
Dentine supports the enamel
Pulp is the soft tissue inside the central cavity
Gum forms a tight collar around the base of the crown
Root
Cement layer secures the root of the tooth in position
Jaw bone
Blood vessels and nerves supply the living pulp tissue

INSIDE A TOOTH
This cross-section of a tooth shows its framework made of bonelike dentine. This forms the tooth's root, which is cemented in the jaw bone. Dentine also supports a rock-hard crown of nonliving enamel for grinding up food. The central cavity contains living pulp tissue and the blood vessels that feed it, and nerve endings, which sense pressure to help us bite and chew food.

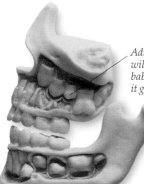

Adult tooth will push out baby tooth as it grows

Root anchors tooth in jaw bone

Upper third molar (wisdom tooth)

FIVE-YEAR TEETH
The first 20 baby teeth appear from the age of six months. From about six years these begin to fall out and are replaced by adult teeth.

FULL SET OF ADULT TEETH
By early adulthood, all 32 adult teeth have come through. Each half jaw has two incisors, one canine, two premolars, and three molars. Some people's third molars (wisdom teeth) never appear.

Digestion

AFTER SWALLOWING, IT TAKES 10 SECONDS for lumps of chewed food to arrive in the stomach. Digestion This really gets digestion underway. Digestion breaks down food into the nutrients that are used by body cells. First the stomach begins to break food down with enzymes (chemical digesters) and churns it into liquid chyme, which it releases slowly into the small intestine. Here, bile (a fluid from the liver) and pancreatic juice make the chyme less acid, while further enzymes digest food into its simplest components—glucose (sugar), amino acids, and fatty acids. These nutrients are then absorbed into the bloodstream. The leftover waste passes through the large intestine, which removes water to maintain the body's water levels. Some waste is digested by the trillions of bacteria that live in the large intestine, providing the body with further nutrients, such as vitamin K.

FOOD-PROCESSING STOMACH

The stomach is a J-shaped bag that expands as it receives recently swallowed food through the esophagus (gullet). The stomach then stores and processes this food for the next few hours. Its muscular wall contracts powerfully to churn up food, while acidic gastric (stomach) juice digests the food's proteins. The end result is a soupy liquid called chyme. This is released slowly into the small intestine.

Esophagus

Stomach has a muscular wall

Transverse colon conceals the duodenum connecting the stomach to the jejunum

Jejunum is the middle section of the small intestine

Descending colon

Left lobe of the liver

THE BODY'S CHEMICAL FACTORY

The liver is the body's largest internal organ. It is made up of cells called hepatocytes. These perform over 500 functions, which help to balance and maintain the chemical makeup of blood. The liver receives oxygen-rich blood from the heart, and blood rich in nutrients from the intestines. As blood flows past hepatocytes, nutrients are either released into the bloodstream for circulation, or stored for future use. Other liver functions include making bile (see below), removing poisons from the blood, destroying bacteria, and recycling worn-out red blood cells. All this chemical activity generates heat, which helps keep the body warm.

Right lobe of the liver

Gall bladder stores bile

Ascending colon

THE INTESTINES

The small intestine is around 20 ft (6 m) long and has three sections. The short duodenum receives chyme from the stomach and digestive fluids (bile and pancreatic juice) from the liver and pancreas. The jejunum and the ileum are where digestion is completed and nutrients are absorbed. Because the small intestine's lining is folded and covered by tiny, finger-like villi, it provides a huge surface for absorption. The large intestine is shorter, just 1.5 m (5 ft) long, and consists of the cecum, the colon, and the rectum. Watery waste from the ileum dries out as it passes

PIT OF THE STOMACH

This SEM shows the gastric (stomach) pits in close-up. Millions of these tiny holes dot the stomach's lining and lead to the gastric glands. The glands release gastric juice—a mixture of hydrochloric acid, pepsinogen, and mucus—into the stomach. Here, the acid converts pepsinogen into pepsin, an enzyme that digests the proteins in food. The mucus coats the stomach lining and prevents gastric juice from

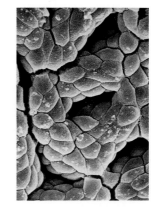

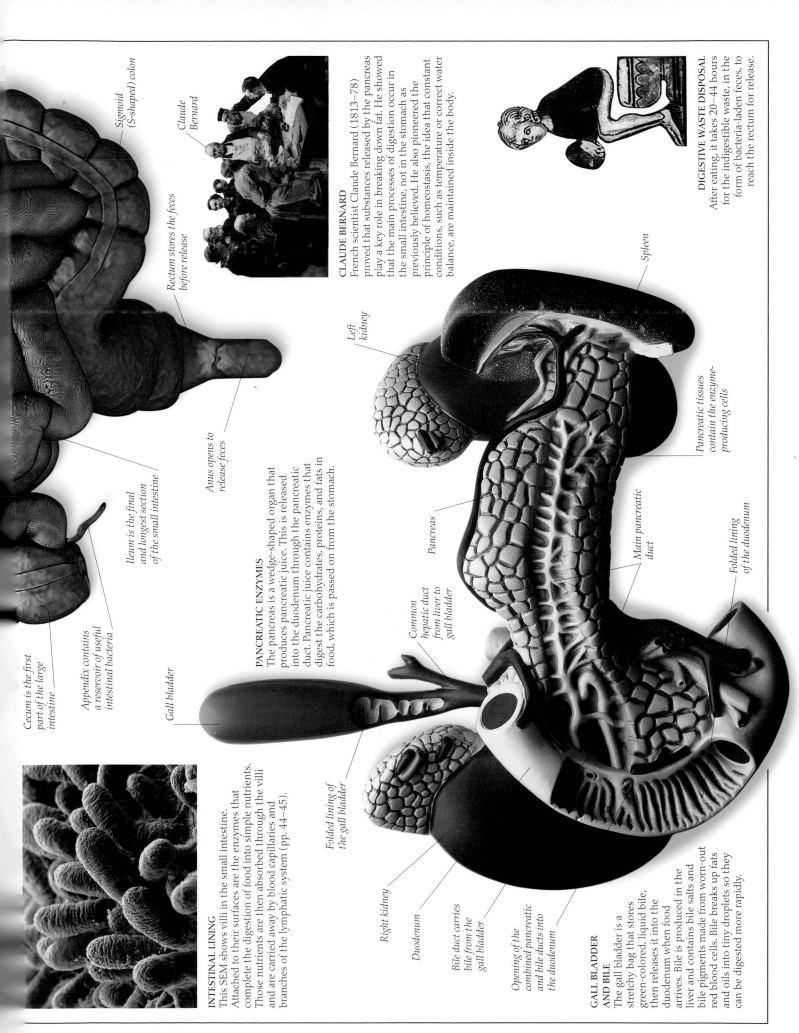

Sigmoid (S-shaped) colon

Claude Bernard

Rectum stores the feces before release

CLAUDE BERNARD
French scientist Claude Bernard (1813–78) proved that substances released by the pancreas play a key role in breaking down fat. He showed that the main processes of digestion occur in the small intestine, not in the stomach as previously believed. He also pioneered the principle of homeostasis, the idea that constant conditions, such as temperature or correct water balance, are maintained inside the body.

DIGESTIVE WASTE DISPOSAL
After eating, it takes 20–44 hours for the indigestible waste, in the form of bacteria-laden feces, to reach the rectum for release.

Cecum is the first part of the large intestine

Appendix contains a reservoir of useful intestinal bacteria

Ileum is the final and longest section of the small intestine

Anus opens to release feces

PANCREATIC ENZYMES
The pancreas is a wedge-shaped organ that produces pancreatic juice. This is released into the duodenum through the pancreatic duct. Pancreatic juice contains enzymes that digest the carbohydrates, proteins, and fats in food, which is passed on from the stomach.

INTESTINAL LINING
This SEM shows villi in the small intestine. Attached to their surfaces are the enzymes that complete the digestion of food into simple nutrients. Those nutrients are then absorbed through the villi and are carried away by blood capillaries and branches of the lymphatic system (pp. 44–45).

Left kidney

Spleen

Pancreatic tissues contain the enzyme-producing cells

Pancreas

Main pancreatic duct

Folded lining of the duodenum

Common hepatic duct from liver to gall bladder

Gall bladder

Folded lining of the gall bladder

Right kidney

Duodenum

Bile duct carries bile from the gall bladder

Opening of the combined pancreatic and bile ducts into the duodenum

GALL BLADDER AND BILE
The gall bladder is a stretchy bag that stores green-colored, liquid bile, then releases it into the duodenum when food arrives. Bile is produced in the liver and contains bile salts and bile pigments made from worn-out red blood cells. Bile breaks up fats and oils into tiny droplets so they can be digested more rapidly.

Waste disposal

BODY CELLS ARE CONTINUALLY releasing waste substances, such as urea made by the liver, into the bloodstream. If these wastes were left to build up, they would end up poisoning the body. The urinary system disposes of waste by cleansing the blood as it passes through a pair of kidneys. It also removes excess water to ensure that the body's water content always remains the same. Inside each kidney, microscopic filtering units remove the wastes in blood but retain useful substances such as nutrients. Wastes are combined with water to form urine, which travels down two long tubes, called ureters, to the bladder. This organ stores the urine and then passes it out through the urethra as a person urinates.

BLADDER CONTROL
When a baby's bladder is full of urine, the stretch receptors in its muscular wall automatically tell it to empty. Young children gradually learn to control this reflex action.

GIANT OF ANCIENT GREECE
The learned Greek philosopher Aristotle (384–322 BCE) is known as the father of nature and biology. Aristotle questioned the traditional anatomical teachings of his day, by looking inside the real bodies of animals and humans and recording what he saw. His books provided the first descriptions of the urinary system and how it works.

Kidney cortex contains blood capillaries and Bowman's capsules

Nephron (filtering unit) consists of a glomerulus and a looping tubule

Capillary reabsorbs nutrients and water from the tubule

Glomerulus inside a Bowman's capsule filters blood

Bowman's capsule

Medulla contains blood vessels and urine-forming tubules

Tubule

U-shaped loop of Henle

Collecting duct

CAPSULES AND LOOPS
William Bowman (1816–92) was an English anatomist, histologist (expert in body tissues), and surgeon. He identified the capsule that bears his name in 1842. The U-shaped loop of Henle was described 20 years later by the German anatomist Jakob Henle (1809–85).

William Bowman

Small artery entering the glomerulus

Small arte[ry] leaving th[e] glomerulu[s]

Space where filtered fluid collects

Capillary of the glomerulus

Start of tubule

FILTERING UNIT
The kidney's blood filtering unit, called a nephron, consists of a glomerulus inside a Bowman's capsule connected to a long tubule. The tubule loops from the cortex down to the medulla and back to the cortex before joining a collecting duct. As fluid filtered from blood passes along the nephron, useful substances are absorbed back into the bloodstream, leaving waste urine to flow into the collecting duct.

INSIDE A BOWMAN'S CAPSULE
Each cup-shaped Bowman's capsule surrounds a glomerulus, or a cluster of capillaries. The capillaries filter the blood and produce a fluid, which collects in the space inside the capsule. This fluid contains not only waste, but also substances such as glucose (sugar), which are useful to the body.

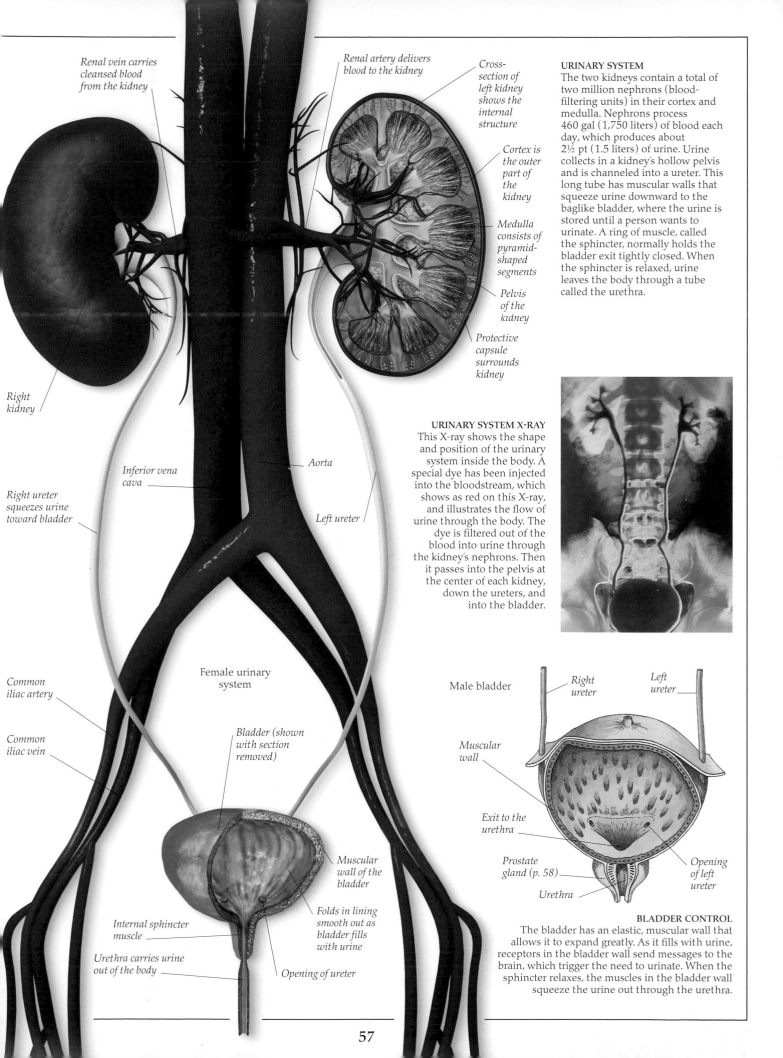

Renal vein carries
cleansed blood
from the kidney

Renal artery delivers
blood to the kidney

Cross-
section of
left kidney
shows the
internal
structure

URINARY SYSTEM
The two kidneys contain a total of
two million nephrons (blood-
filtering units) in their cortex and
medulla. Nephrons process
460 gal (1,750 liters) of blood each
day, which produces about
2½ pt (1.5 liters) of urine. Urine
collects in a kidney's hollow pelvis
and is channeled into a ureter. This
long tube has muscular walls that
squeeze urine downward to the
baglike bladder, where the urine is
stored until a person wants to
urinate. A ring of muscle, called
the sphincter, normally holds the
bladder exit tightly closed. When
the sphincter is relaxed, urine
leaves the body through a tube
called the urethra.

Cortex is
the outer
part of
the
kidney

Medulla
consists of
pyramid-
shaped
segments

Pelvis
of the
kidney

Protective
capsule
surrounds
kidney

Right
kidney

Right ureter
squeezes urine
toward bladder

Inferior vena
cava

Aorta

Left ureter

URINARY SYSTEM X-RAY
This X-ray shows the shape
and position of the urinary
system inside the body. A
special dye has been injected
into the bloodstream, which
shows as red on this X-ray,
and illustrates the flow of
urine through the body. The
dye is filtered out of the
blood into urine through
the kidney's nephrons. Then
it passes into the pelvis at
the center of each kidney,
down the ureters, and
into the bladder.

Common
iliac artery

Common
iliac vein

Female urinary
system

Male bladder

Right
ureter

Left
ureter

Bladder (shown
with section
removed)

Muscular
wall

Muscular
wall of the
bladder

Exit to the
urethra

Folds in lining
smooth out as
bladder fills
with urine

Prostate
gland (p. 58)

Opening
of left
ureter

Internal sphincter
muscle

Urethra

Urethra carries urine
out of the body

Opening of ureter

BLADDER CONTROL
The bladder has an elastic, muscular wall that
allows it to expand greatly. As it fills with urine,
receptors in the bladder wall send messages to the
brain, which trigger the need to urinate. When the
sphincter relaxes, the muscles in the bladder wall
squeeze the urine out through the urethra.

Male and female

HUMANS HAVE A LIMITED lifespan and, like all life-forms, they reproduce to pass on their genes and continue the cycle of life. Male and female reproductive systems are different from each other. The process of reproduction requires both sexes—a man and a woman—to produce sex cells, which must join together in order to produce a new human being. The male reproductive system consists of the penis and the testes, and the tubes and glands that connect them. The testes make tadpole-shaped sex cells called spermatozoa (sperm). The female reproductive system is made up of the ovaries, fallopian tubes, uterus, and vagina. The ovaries make and release spherical sex cells called ova (eggs). Sexual intercourse (sex) between a man and a woman brings the eggs and sperm together. These sex cells contain half of each partner's DNA (genetic instructions), which combine during fertilization inside the woman's body to create a new life. The woman's uterus then provides the place where the resulting baby will develop.

MALE AND FEMALE FORMS
These male and female human figures are from *Epitome,* a guide to anatomy published by Andreas Vesalius in 1543. The illustrations of external features show that the male is more muscular than the female, with wide shoulders, narrow hips, and more facial and body hair. The female's overall contours are rounded by pads of body fat, particularly around the thighs and abdomen, with wide hips and developed breasts.

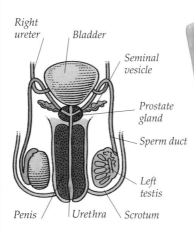

Right ureter *Bladder*

Seminal vesicle

Prostate gland

Sperm duct

Left testis

Penis *Urethra* *Scrotum*

Front view of the male reproductive system

MALE REPRODUCTIVE ORGANS
This cross-section model of the male reproductive system shows a side view of one of the two testes, which hang outside the body in a skin bag, called the scrotum. Inside each testis, a hormone stimulates sperm production. During sex, muscle contractions push sperm along two sperm ducts into the urethra and out of the penis. A man makes sperm throughout his adult life. If sperm are not released, they are broken down and reabsorbed.

Bladder

Urethra

Penis

Left testis

Scrotum

Epididymis

Seminal vesicle, together with the prostate gland, adds fluid to the sperm to nourish and stimulate them

Prostate gland

REGNIER DE GRAAF

Dutch physician and anatomist Regnier de Graaf (1641–73) conducted detailed research on the male and female reproductive systems. In his work on the female reproductive organs, published in 1672, de Graaf identified the ovaries. In particular he described the tiny bubbles on the ovary's surface that appear each month. Later it was discovered that each bubble is a ripe follicle with the much smaller egg contained within it. These were named Graafian follicles in de Graaf's honor.

THE MENSTRUAL CYCLE

Every 28 days, a woman's reproductive system undergoes a sequence of changes called the menstrual (monthly) cycle, or period. This controls the release of a mature egg from an ovary. It also thickens the lining of the uterus to receive the egg if it is fertilized by a sperm. The menstrual cycle is controlled by hormones released by the pituitary gland (pp. 40–41) and the ovaries.

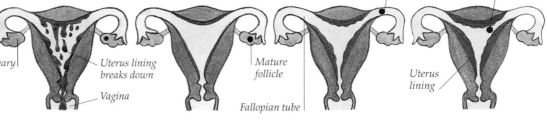

Ovary

Uterus lining breaks down

Vagina

Mature follicle

Fallopian tube

Egg

Egg

Uterus lining

1 FIRST WEEK
The uterus lining, which thickened during the previous menstrual cycle, breaks down and is lost as blood-flow through the vagina.

2 SECOND WEEK
An egg-containing follicle near the ovary's surface ripens to become a mature (Graafian) follicle. The uterus lining begins to grow and thicken again.

3 THIRD WEEK
Midmonth, ovulation occurs when the mature follicle bursts open and releases its egg. The egg is moved along the fallopian tube toward the uterus.

4 FOURTH WEEK
The uterus lining is thick and blood-rich. If the egg has been fertilized it sinks into the lining. If not, it is broken down and the cycle begins again.

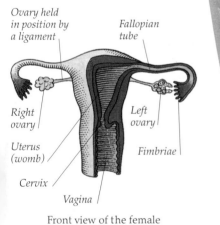

Ovary held in position by a ligament

Fallopian tube

Right ovary

Left ovary

Uterus (womb)

Fimbriae

Cervix

Vagina

Front view of the female reproductive system

FEMALE REPRODUCTIVE ORGANS

A woman's ovaries release a single mature egg each month during her fertile years. When an egg is released by an ovary, it is wafted by fimbriae into the fallopian tube that leads to the uterus. If the egg meets a sperm soon after its release, the two fuse and fertilization occurs, resulting in a baby that grows inside the uterus (womb). If fertilization does not occur, the egg is reabsorbed. As the baby develops, the uterus expands greatly. The vagina is the tube through which the baby is eventually born.

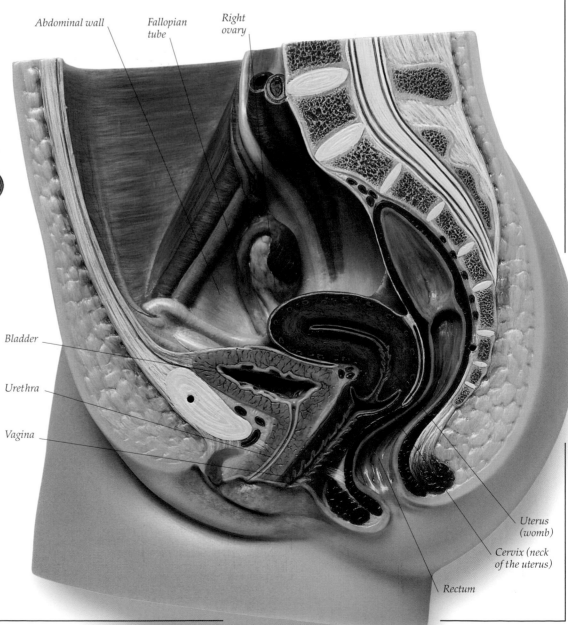

Abdominal wall

Fallopian tube

Right ovary

Bladder

Urethra

Vagina

Uterus (womb)

Cervix (neck of the uterus)

Rectum

A new life

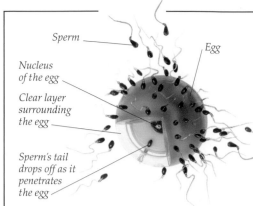

FERTILIZATION OF AN EGG

This cutaway model shows sperm clustered around an egg. Each sperm consists of a head, containing its nucleus, and a tail that propels it. These sperm are trying to get through the outer covering of the egg. One has succeeded, its tail has dropped off, and its head (nucleus) will fuse with, or fertilize, the egg's nucleus. No other sperm can now penetrate the egg.

Sperm

Egg

Nucleus of the egg

Clear layer surrounding the egg

Sperm's tail drops off as it penetrates the egg

THE ACT OF FERTILIZATION merges the DNA (genetic instructions) carried by a male sperm and female egg. The result is a fertilized egg, no bigger than the period at the end of this sentence. If the fertilized egg successfully implants itself in the lining of the woman's uterus, it grows first into an embryo and then a fetus. Around 38 weeks after fertilization, changes in the mother's body signal that the fetus is ready to be born. The muscular wall of the uterus starts to contract. As the contractions get stronger and more frequent the membranes surrounding the fetus tear, releasing the amniotic fluid in which the baby floated. The cervix of the uterus widens and the baby is pushed out through its mother's vagina. Contact with the outside world stimulates the newborn baby to take its first breaths. In the years that follow, the child will need the care and nurturing of its parents as it grows and develops.

EMBRYO DEVELOPMENT

The fertilized egg divides into two cells, then into four, then eight, and so on. A week after fertilization, it implants in the lining of the uterus, becoming an embryo. As they divide, the embryo's cells form muscle, nerve, and other tissues. Five weeks after fertilization, the pea-sized embryo's arms and legs are already developing, as are its internal organs.

Cluster of 16 cells

Model of a five-week-old embryo

Heart

Arm bud

Ear beginning to form

Developing eye

Developing mouth

Tail bud

Leg bud

Developing vertebra of the spine (backbone)

Liver can be seen

FIRST EMBRYOLOGIST

In 1600, Italian anatomy professor Hieronymus Fabricius (1537–1619) published *On the Formation of the Fetus*, which described the development of unborn babies in a range of animals, including humans. Even in his lifetime, Fabricius was known as the founder of embryology, for his study of embryos and their development. He also named the ovary, and predicted its function.

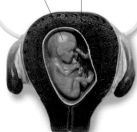

Uterus enlarges to accommodate the growing fetus

Recognizable limbs

Uterus wall

All main organs are formed

Umbilical cord

Cervix

Placenta

FETAL DEVELOPMENT

From two months after fertilization through to birth, the developing baby gradually comes to look distinctly human. It is now known as a fetus, from the Latin word for "offspring." At two months, all of the major organs have formed, and the fetal heart is beating, yet its body is still just the size of a strawberry. By around nine months, when it is ready to be born, the fetus weighs about 6½–9 lb (3–4 kg).

1 TWO MONTHS
The 1-in- (2.5-mm-) long fetus has arms and legs, fingers and toes. Its brain is expanding rapidly.

2 THREE MONTHS
About 3 in (8 cm) long, the fetus is recognizably human, with eyes on its face.

3 FIVE MONTHS
The fetus is 8 in (20 cm) long, and responds to sounds by kicking and turning somersaults. The mother's abdomen bulges.

THE PLACENTA
The placenta is a disk of tissue that is joined to the wall of the uterus and nourishes the fetus. Inside it, blood vessels from the mother and fetus pass very close to each other. This allows oxygen and food to pass from the mother's blood into the blood of the fetus. The fetus's blood flows into and out of the placenta through blood vessels in the umbilical cord. The waste produced by the fetus flows in the opposite direction. After the baby is born, the umbilical cord is clamped and cut. The placenta detaches and is delivered though the vagina.

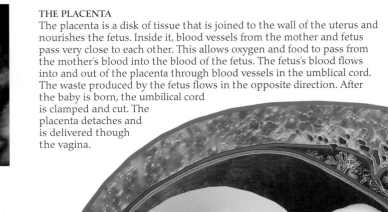

Fetal blood vessels

Maternal blood vessel

Placenta forms a link between the baby's blood and its mother's blood

Umbilical arteries

SEEING THE FETUS
Ultrasound scans of babies developing in the uterus are performed after about 11 weeks, to check that all is well with the fetus. An ultrasound scanner beams very high-pitched, but harmless, sound waves into the body, and detects their echoes. A computer displays the echoes as an image on a screen. In this detailed 3-D scan, the fetus is holding its left hand up to its forehead.

Blood vessels inside the umbilical cord carry blood to and from the fetus

Fetus has grown visibly in the past two months

Expanded uterus presses on the mother's abdominal organs

Stretched uterus wall

Cervical plug made of thick mucus blocks the cervix to protect the fetus from infection

Cervix

Vagina (birth canal)

Amniotic fluid

Amnion is the membrane containing amniotic fluid in which the baby floats

Fetus has turned upside down into the birth position

Cervix tightly shut

4 SEVEN MONTHS
The fetus is now about 16 in (28 cm) long, and is cramped inside the uterus. It has finger and toenails, and its eyes are open.

5 NINE MONTHS
The fetus is now fully grown, at about 14 in (36 cm) long. It responds to music and voices, has fully formed lungs, and is ready to be born.

MOTHER AND BABY
Many mothers breast-feed their babies. Breast milk supplies the baby with the nutrients required for growth and development in the early months before it can eat solid food. Milk is produced by glands inside the breasts and released when the baby suckles. Breastfeeding also forms part of the bonding process between mother and child.

Growth and development

THROUGHOUT LIFE, FROM BIRTH TO OLD AGE, every human follows the same pattern of growth and body development. A new baby has a relatively large head and brain and short limbs. The torso (chest and abdomen) catches up during childhood, and the arms and legs are the last to lengthen during the teenage years. It is in these teenage years that physical and mental changes cause the move from childhood to adulthood. By a person's early 20s, growth has stopped. The body then matures, and in later years begins to deteriorate. This pattern, like all of the body's processes, is controlled by 23 pairs of chromosomes inside the nucleus of every body cell. Each chromosome is made of a long molecule called deoxyribonucleic acid (DNA). Sections of each DNA molecule, called genes, contain the coded instructions required to build and maintain a human being. The complete set of instructions consists of around 25,000 pairs of genes.

MASTER MOLECULE
In 1953, US biologist James Watson (1928–) (shown on left) with British biophysicist Francis Crick (1916–2004) discovered the structure of DNA. This photograph shows the pair with their DNA molecular model. It has two linked, parallel strands that spiral around each other like a twisted ladder. The rungs of this ladder hold the code that forms the instructions in genes.

GENES AND INHERITANCE
When a man and woman reproduce, they each pass on a set of genes to their child. This passing on of DNA instructions is called inheritance. The genes that this girl inherited from her mother and father are mostly identical, but some are different. This gives her a unique combination of genes, some of which determine her individual traits, such as her physical appearance or athletic ability. This girl may have inherited her dark hair and brown eyes from her mother but she remains different from both her parents.

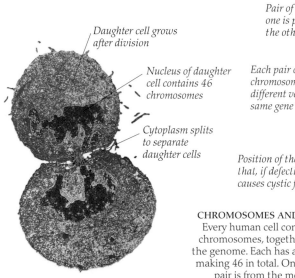

Daughter cell grows after division

Nucleus of daughter cell contains 46 chromosomes

Cytoplasm splits to separate daughter cells

CELL DIVISION
Human growth requires our bodies to make new cells. Cells reproduce by dividing in two. For most cells, division involves a process called mitosis, where each chromosome duplicates inside a parent cell to produce an identical copy. The two sets of chromosomes line up and then move to opposite ends of the cell's cytoplasm. Finally, the cytoplasm divides to produce two daughter cells that are identical to each other.

Banding pattern on every chromosome is produced by chemicals and used in mapping

Sex chromosome Y is passed on by the father

XY sex chromosomes determine that this person is male. An XX pairing would make the person female

Pair of matching chromosomes: one is passed on by the mother, the other by the father

Sex chromosome X is passed on by the father or mother

Each pair of matching chromosomes may carry different versions of the same gene

Position of the gene, that, if defective, causes cystic fibrosis

CHROMOSOMES AND GENES
Every human cell contains 23 chromosomes, together called the genome. Each has a partner, making 46 in total. One of each pair is from the mother, the other from the father. Each chromosome has the same genes as its partner, but it might not carry identical versions. It might carry the version of a gene giving blue eyes, but the other chromosome might have the version for brown. Twenty-two of the chromosome pairs match. The twenty-third pair matches only in females and determines a person's sex. In 2003, the Human Genome Project identified the sequence of chemical bases (p. 7) on the entire genome. This knowledge is helping scientists map the location of specific genes.

Map of the genome of a man

Chromosome 12 carries over 1,400 genes

3 2 1 Y X 22
4 21
5 20
6 19
7 18
8 17
9 16
10 15
11 12 13 14

GROWTH AND THE SKELETON

Before birth, the embryo's skeleton is made up of either flexible cartilage or, in the case of the skull, membranes reinforced with fibers. As the fetus grows, most of these tissues are replaced by hard bone, a process called ossification. At birth, however, the bones of the cranium (skull) are incomplete. They are connected by fontanelles, or flexible membranes, that allow the baby's head to be slightly squashed to ease the birth, and later for the brain to grow. By early childhood, the fontanelles are ossified, and the skull bones are knitted together at jigsawlike joints called sutures. During childhood, the skull's facial bones grow rapidly to catch up with the cranium.

Anterior fontanelle

Mastoid fontanelle

Sphenoidal fontanelle

Fetal skull

Small facial bones

PUBERTY AND ADOLESCENCE

During the three to four years of puberty, the body grows rapidly and the reproductive system begins to function. Most girls reach puberty at 10–12 years, and boys at 12–14 years. A girl's body becomes more rounded, she develops breasts, and her periods start. A boy's body becomes more muscular, his voice deepens, facial hair grows, and he starts producing sperm. Puberty forms part of adolescence, the process that changes a child into an adult. Adolescence involves mental changes as well as physical ones and it can be a time of worry, rebellion, and new-found independence. In the film *Rebel Without a Cause* (1955), the character played by actor James Dean perfectly illustrates the brooding teenage years.

Cranial bones has ossified completely

Facial bones grow rapidly during childhood

Adult tooth pushing out the baby tooth

Lower jaw greatly increased in size

Jigsawlike, fixed suture joint

Six-year-old skull

LATER YEARS

From about the age of 50, aging of the body becomes noticeable. The skin loses its springiness and develops lines and wrinkles, as seen in the face of this elderly Native American. Inside the body, the heart and lungs become less efficient, joints stiffen, bones become more fragile, vision is less effective, and brain function decreases. However, these changes may happen more slowly if people care for their bodies. Healthy food and exercise may help people enjoy good health well into their 80s.

Chief of the Crow tribe (c. 1906)

Adult skull

Suture joints still visible in adult skull

Young adulthood

Middle age

Old age

Puberty and adolescence

Birth

Death

Facial bones have grown larger still

Tooth missing, possibly from decay

LIFE STORY FROM CRADLE TO GRAVE

Every human follows the same life story, as this 16th-century illustration shows. Following birth and childhood, a child becomes an adult in the teenage years. Early adulthood is a time of responsibility and becoming a parent. Middle age brings wisdom but also the start of aging. In old age, the body's workings begin to decline until, eventually, the person dies. Today, thanks to better food, health care, and sanitation in the developed world, average life expectancy is approaching 80 years, twice that of the 16th century.

Future bodies

Stem cells taken
from umbilical
cord blood

ADVANCES IN THE FIELDS of biology, medicine, electronics, and technology are making it possible to repair or improve the human body in ways previously thought impossible. Some people raise moral objections to research using stem cells or hybrid embryos, believing that these techniques interfere with the sanctity of life. No such objections are raised against bionic limbs or the growth of artificial organs. Today's notions of nanobots, cyborgs, and brain microchips still remain dreams for the future.

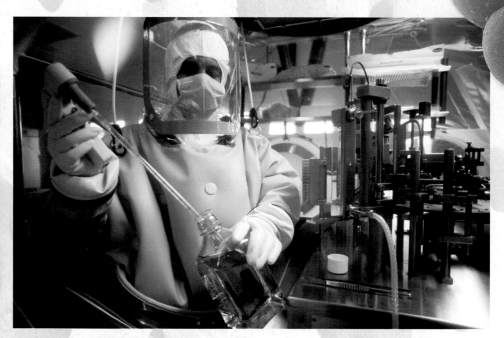

STEM CELLS
Doctors believe that unspecialized cells, called stem cells, can be used to repair diseased or damaged tissues in patients Stem cells divide to produce a range of cell types and so can build many types of body tissue. The most adaptable stem cells are taken for research from specially created embryos. However, some people object to this practice. Stem cells are also collected from umbilical cord blood and used to produce various types of blood cells.

GENE THERAPY
Each body cell contains over 20,000 genes, the DNA instructions that build and run it. A faulty gene that does not do its job properly can cause disease. Research scientists (above) hope that it will soon be possible to cure some conditions using gene therapy. This technique replaces faulty genes with normal ones. A harmless virus is used to carry a normal version of the gene into body cells to correct the error.

DESIGNER CHILDREN
In the future, it may be possible to treat a sick child with a faulty gene by using stem cells obtained from a specially designed sibling. First, a number of embryos are created through the medical technique of in vitro fertilization (IVF), where an egg is fertilized outside the body in a laboratory. One embryo is then selected if its cells match those of its sibling, and if it does not have the same genetic fault. This embryo is placed in the mother's uterus to develop into a baby. When the designer child is born, stem cells in its discarded umbilical cord are used to treat its sick sibling.

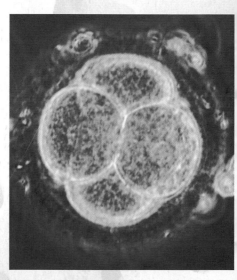

HYBRID EMBRYOS
Embryos are a source of stem cells, but the human eggs needed to make them are a scarce resource. Scientists may therefore create hybrid embryos. In a hybrid embryo, the nucleus that contains DNA is removed from a cow's egg and replaced by a nucleus from a human skin cell. The resulting cell divides to create a hybrid embryo that is 99.9 percent human. The stem cells are then harvested from the embryo and used to research cures for diseases.

Bionic arm is wired to the chest muscles

Sensors monitor signals from the chest muscles and trigger arm and hand movements

Artificial hand and fingers move according to the woman's conscious thoughts

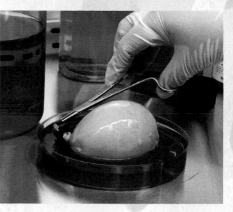

Neuron is one of a network forming a circuit with a microchip

Pillar supports the neuron on the microchip

BIONIC LIMBS

This patient lost her left arm in a motorcycle accident. She is one of the first people to be fitted with a thought-controlled bionic arm. Surgeons wired the bionic arm to her chest muscles. When she thinks about moving her hand, messages travel to her chest muscles, which send out electrical signals. These are detected by electronic sensors and passed on to a tiny computer that tells her hand how to move.

GROWING ORGANS

Currently, diseased organs can be replaced only by transplanting a donor organ from another person. An alternative solution for the future might be to grow new organs in a laboratory. This technique has already been tested using bladder cells from a patient. First, bladder tissue was grown around a mold (see above) and then the new bladder was successfully implanted into the patient.

BRAIN MICROCHIPS

This SEM shows one of a network of human neurons (nerve cells) on a microchip. Microchips are miniature electronic circuits. This microchip is forming a circuit with the neurons and can stimulate them to send and receive signals to one another and to the microchip. Future scientists may succeed in using neuron–microchip circuits to repair brain damage, or perhaps to enhance abilities such as memory or intelligence.

MEDICAL NANOBOTS

This artwork shows a futuristic scene of a medical nanobot examining nerve cells. Nanobots, or nanorobots, are microscopic machines that are self-propelled, respond to their surroundings, and are able to carry out tasks using their own initiative. They are created by nanotechnology, the manipulation of atoms and molecules to build tiny machines. In the future, it may be possible for medical nanobots to detect, diagnose, and repair damage to the body's cells and tissues.

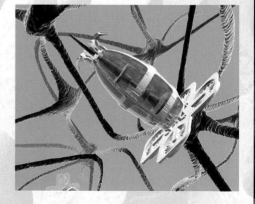

CYBORGS

In the *Terminator* films, actor Arnold Schwarzenegger (left) played the role of a cyborg—a character with increased natural abilities, being part human and part machine. Future technological advances may yet make cyborgs a reality and enable humans to keep pace with increasingly intelligent robots and other artificial systems.

ETERNAL LIFE?

Some scientists and philosophers—the people who study life and its meaning—predict that the average human lifespan could be extended to 150 years. Medical advances, such as gene therapy and organ replacement, together with lifestyle changes could enable everyone to live longer. But, what quality of life would there be for a 150-year-old? And is there room on our already crowded planet for so many extra, possibly unproductive, human beings?

Timeline

Our **detailed knowledge** of anatomy and physiology comes from the in-depth study and contributions of scientists and doctors through the ages. With each new discovery, following generations were able to build up an ever clearer picture of the body and its systems. Even so, there remain many mysteries about the workings of the human body that have yet to be understood.

Statue of Imhotep c. 2650 BCE

c. 160,000 BCE
Modern humans (*Homo sapiens*) first appear in Africa.

c. 10,000 BCE
Earliest settled communities and the beginnings of agriculture.

c. 2650 BCE
Egyptian Imhotep is the earliest known physician.

c. 1500 BCE
The earliest known medical text, the *Ebers Papyrus*, is written in Egypt.

c. 500 BCE
Greek physician Alcmaeon of Croton suggests that the brain, not the heart, is the seat of thought and feelings.

c. 420 BCE
Greek physician Hippocrates emphasizes the importance of observation and diagnosis.

c. 280 BCE
Herophilus of Alexandria describes the cerebrum and cerebellum of the brain.

40 CE
Roman philosopher Cornelius Celsus publishes the medical handbook *On Medicine*.

c. 200 CE
Greek-born Roman doctor Claudius Galen describes, often incorrectly, the workings of the human body; his teachings will remain unchallenged until the 1500s.

c. 1025
Persian doctor Avicenna publishes the *Canon of Medicine*, which will influence European medicine for the next 500 years.

c. 1280
Syrian doctor Ibn an-Nafis shows that blood circulates around the body.

c. 1316
Italian anatomy professor Mondino dei Liuzzi publishes his dissection guide *Anatomy*.

c. 1500
Italian artist and scientist Leonardo da Vinci makes anatomical drawings based on his own dissections, not Galen's teachings.

1543
Flemish doctor Andreas Vesalius publishes *On the Structure of the Human Body*, which accurately describes human anatomy.

1562
Italian anatomist Bartolomeo Eustachio describes the ear in *The Examination of the Organ of Hearing*.

1590
Dutch spectacle maker, Zacharias Janssen, invents the microscope.

1603
Hieronymus Fabricius, an Italian anatomist, describes the structure of a vein in his book, *On the Valves of Veins*.

1614
Italian physician Santorio Santorio publishes the findings of his 30-year-long study of his own body in *The Art of Statistical Medicine*.

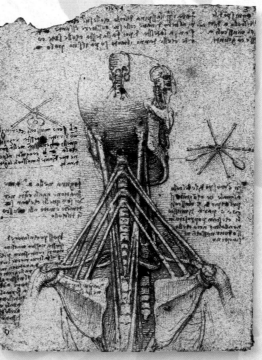

Anatomical drawing by Leonardo da Vinci, c. 1500

1628
English doctor William Harvey describes blood circulation in his work *On the Movement of the Heart and Blood in Animals*.

1662
French philosopher René Descartes' posthumously published book, *Treatise of Man*, describes the human body as a machine.

1663
Italian biologist Marcello Malpighi discovers capillaries, the small blood vessels that link arteries and veins.

1664
English doctor Thomas Willis describes the blood supply to the brain.

1665
English physicist Robert Hooke coins the term "cell" to describe the smallest units of life he observes through his compound microscope.

Hooke's microscope, 1665

1672
Dutch anatomist Regnier de Graaf describes the female reproductive system.

1674–77
Antoni van Leeuwenhoek, a Dutch cloth merchant and microscopist, describes human blood cells and sperm cells.

1691
English doctor Clopton Havers describes the microscopic structure of bones.

1775
French chemist Antoine Lavoisier discovers oxygen and later shows that cell respiration is a chemical process that consumes oxygen.

1800
French doctor Marie-François Bichat shows that organs are made of groups of cells called tissues.

1811
Scottish anatomist Charles Bell shows that nerves are bundles of nerve cells.

1816
French doctor René Laënnec invents the stethoscope, used for listening to breathing and heart sounds.

1833
American army surgeon William Beaumont publishes the results of his experiments into the mechanism of digestion.

1837
Czech biologist Johannes Purkinje observes neurons in the cerebellum of the brain.

1842
British surgeon William Bowman describes the microscopic structure and workings of the kidney.

1848
French scientist Claude Bernard describes the workings of the liver.

An early ophthalmoscope

1851
German physicist Hermann von Helmholtz invents the ophthalmoscope, an instrument for looking inside the eye.

1861
French doctor Paul Pierre Broca identifies the area on the left side of the brain that controls speech.

1871
German scientist Wilhelm Kühne invents the term "enzyme" to describe substances that accelerate chemical reactions inside living things.

1895
German physicist Wilhelm Roentgen discovers X-rays.

1901
Karl Landsteiner, an Austrian-American doctor, identifies blood groups, paving the way for more successful blood transfusions.

1905
British scientist Ernest Starling devises the term "hormone" to describe the body's chemical messengers.

1930
American physiologist Walter Cannon devises the term "homeostasis" to describe mechanisms that maintain a stable state inside the body.

1933
German electrical engineer Ernst Ruska invents the electron microscope.

1952
US surgeon Joseph E. Murray performs the first kidney transplant. The operation was performed on identical twins.

A wounded US soldier receives a blood transfusion during World War II

1952
US heart specialist Paul Zoll develops the first cardiac pacemaker to control an irregular heartbeat.

1953
US biologist James Watson and British physicist Francis Crick discover the double-helix structure of DNA.

1958
British doctor Ian Donald uses ultrasound scanning to check the health of a fetus.

1961
American scientist Marshall Nirenberg cracks the genetic code of DNA.

1967
Magnetic resonance imaging (MRI) is first used to see soft tissues inside the body.

1972
Computed tomography (CT) scanning is introduced to produce images of human body organs.

1980
Doctors perform "keyhole" surgery operations inside the body through small incisions with the assistance of an endoscope.

1980s
Positron emission tomography (PET) scans are first used to produce images of brain activity.

Blood bag

1982
The first artificial heart, invented by US scientist Robert Jarvik, is transplanted into a patient.

1984
French scientist Luc Montagnier discovers the human immunodeficiency virus (HIV) that destroys immune system cells, resulting in AIDS.

1990
The Human Genome Project is launched with the goal of identifying all the genes in human chromosomes.

1999
Chromosome 22 becomes the first human chromosome to have its DNA sequenced (p. 62).

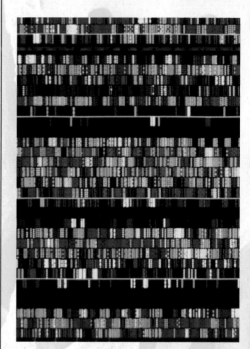

Computer display of DNA sequencing

2001
Scientists perform first germline gene transfer in animals with the goal of preventing faulty genes from being passed on to the next generation.

2002
Gene therapy (p. 64) is used to treat boys suffering from an inherited immunodeficiency disease that leaves the body unable to fight against infection.

2003
Scientists publish results of the Human Genome Project (p. 62), identifying the DNA sequence of a full set of human chromosomes.

2006
A urinary bladder, grown in the laboratory from a patient's own cells, is successfully transplanted into that patient to replace a damaged organ.

2007
Once thought to be a useless organ, the appendix is shown to hold a backup reservoir of bacteria that is essential to the workings of the large intestine.

2008
Dutch geneticist Marjolein Kreik becomes the first woman to have her genome sequenced.

Find out more

THE HUMAN BODY is an endlessly fascinating and absorbing subject. There are many resources available to help you study it further. Listen for news stories about the latest discoveries in medical science, and radio and television documentaries about the human body and how it works. You can find more information about the body in books and on the internet. Keep an eye out for special exhibitions at museums near you that are dedicated to anatomy or physiology. Finally, don't forget, you also have your own body to study! Take good care of it by eating healthily and exercising regularly.

THE OLD OPERATING ROOM
This early 19th-century operating room is located on the original site of St. Thomas' hospital in London. It records a time before anesthetics, when surgeons had to work quickly to minimize a patient's suffering as they performed amputations and other operations. Medical students would observe from the tiered stands surrounding the operating table.

ANATOMY ON SHOW
Body Worlds is a touring display of "plastinates"—real human bodies that are cleverly preserved in exciting poses to reveal inner organs and tissues. The exhibition aims to make anatomy more accessible. Since it first opened in Japan in 1995, more than 20 million people have visited the exhibition worldwide.

One of the plastinates at the *Body Worlds* exhibition

Skin is removed to reveal the muscles, major organs, and blood vessels

WALK-IN BODY

At the Museum of Health and Medical Science in Houston, Texas, visitors can take a larger-than-life tour through the human body, including an arch created by a giant backbone and ribs (above). The *Amazing Body Pavilion* features exciting interactive experiences including a giant eyeball and a walk-through brain, and hands-on exhibits about health and well-being.

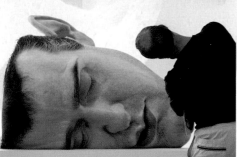

GIANT BODY SCULPTURE

A visitor to Sydney's Museum of Contemporary Art, Australia, studies this lifelike sculpture of a super-sized head. Made from resin and fiberglass, Ron Mueck's *Mask II* is a self-portrait of the artist sleeping. Visits to art galleries to see paintings or sculptures can reveal much about the variety of the human form.

Acrobat's brain controls balance, posture, and precise movements

Muscle and joint flexibility is achieved by constant training

ACROBATICS

Two extraordinarily skillful acrobats from the *Cirque du Soleil* troupe perform as part of the show *Alegría*. Watching circus shows like this provides a great opportunity for us to marvel at the strength, flexibility, and grace of the human body.

Places to visit

HALL OF SCIENCE, NEW YORK, NY
• Infrared camera maps your body's hot spots
• 91 hands-on exhibits that explore perceptions

MUSEUM OF HEALTH AND MEDICAL SCIENCE, HOUSTON, TX
• Outsize displays of body parts, including a 10-ft (3-m) tall walk-through brain
• Over 60 interactive video and audio kiosks

THE FRANKLIN INSTITUTE, PHILADELPHIA, PA
• Giant walk-through heart
• *Melting humans* exhibit shows internal organs

MÜTTER MUSEUM, PHILADELPHIA, PA
• More than 20,000 usual anatomical specimens
• Treasures include a plaster cast of "Siamese twins" and objects removed from people's throats

NATIONAL MUSEUM OF HEALTH AND MEDICINE, WASHINGTON, D.C.
• Preserved specimens from major body systems
• Exhibit on battlefield surgery from the Civil War to Vietnam

HALL OF HEALTH, OAKLAND, CA
• Genetics exhibit with 8 interactive stations
• Electronic quizzes, organ models, and more

MUSEUM OF SCIENCE, BOSTON, MA
• *Human Body Connection* lets you ride a bicycle with a skeleton
• Biotechnology exhibit explains cutting-edge science

CALIFORNIA SCIENCE CENTER, LOS ANGELES, CA
• Giant body simulator shows how the body stays in balance
• 11 preserved embryos and fetuses show the stages of life

SCIENCE MUSEUM OF MINNESOTA, SAINT PAUL, MN
• *Bloodstream Superhighway* pumps simulated blood along a 100 ft (30 m) tube
• Interactive mannequins let kids be the doctors

Early stethoscope on display at the Science Museum, London

USEFUL WEBSITES

• An interactive guide to understanding the human genome
http://www.dnai.org/c/index.html
• A fun, animated guide to the human body
http://www.brainpop.com/health/
• A comprehensive guide to the blood, from platelets to plasma
http://health.howstuffworks.com/blood.htm
• A child-friendly website, with tips on keeping the body healthy
http://kidshealth.org/kid/body/mybody.html
• An exciting website from the BBC covering all aspects of the body
http://www.bbc.co.uk/science/humanbody/

Glossary

Blood vessels supplying the lower arm and hand

ABDOMEN The lower part of the torso between the chest and hips.

ACUPUNCTURE A system of alternative medicine that involves pricking specific areas of the skin with needles to treat various disorders.

ADOLESCENCE The period of physical and mental changes that occur during the teenage years and mark the transition from childhood to adulthood.

ALVEOLI The microscopic air bags in the lungs through which oxygen enters the blood and carbon dioxide leaves it.

AMNIOTIC FLUID A liquid that surrounds the developing fetus inside its mother's uterus. It protects the fetus from knocks and jolts.

ANATOMY The study of the structure of the human body.

ANTIBODY A substance released by lymphocytes (immune system cells) that marks an invading pathogen or germ for destruction.

ARTERY A blood vessel that carries blood from the heart toward the body tissues.

ATOM The smallest particle of an element, such as carbon or hydrogen, that can exist.

BACTERIA A type of microorganism. Some bacteria are pathogens (germs) that cause disease in humans.

BILE A fluid made by the liver and delivered to the intestine. Contains salts that aid digestion.

BLOOD VESSEL A tube, such as an artery, vein, or capillary, that transports blood around the body.

CAPILLARY A microscopic blood vessel that connects arteries to veins.

CARTILAGE A tough, flexible tissue that supports the nose, ears, and other body parts, and covers the ends of bones in joints.

CELL One of the trillions of microscopic living units that make up a human body.

CENTRAL NERVOUS SYSTEM The part of the nervous system made up of the brain and spinal cord.

CHROMOSOME One of 46 packages of DNA found inside most body cells.

CHYME A creamy, souplike liquid made of part-digested food. It forms in the stomach and is released into the small intestine during digestion.

DIAPHRAGM The dome-shaped sheet of muscle separating the thorax from the abdomen.

DIGESTION The breakdown of the complex molecules in food into simple nutrients, such as sugars, which are absorbed into the bloodstream and used by cells.

DISSECTION The careful and methodical cutting open of a dead body to study its internal structure.

DNA (DEOXYRIBONUCLEIC ACID) A molecule containing the genes (instructions) that are needed to build and run the cells of a human body.

EMBALMING A process that preserves a dead body and prevents it from decaying.

EMBRYO The name given to an unborn baby during the first eight weeks of development after fertilization.

ENDOCRINE GLAND A collection of cells, such as those making up the thyroid gland, that release hormones into the bloodstream.

Model of an enzyme involved in the digestion of food

ENZYME A protein that acts as a biological catalyst to speed up the rate of chemical reactions inside and outside cells.

FECES The semisolid waste made up of undigested food, dead cells, and bacteria, removed from the body through the anus.

FERTILIZATION The joining together of a sperm and an egg to make a new human being.

FETUS The name given to a baby growing inside the uterus from its ninth week of development until its birth.

FOLLICLE The cluster of cells inside an ovary that surrounds and nurtures an egg. Also a pit in the skin from which a hair grows.

GAS EXCHANGE The movement of oxygen from the lungs into the bloodstream, and of carbon dioxide from the bloodstream into the lungs.

GENE One of the 20,000–25,000 instructions contained within a cell's chromosomes that control its construction and operation.

GLAND A group of cells that create chemical substances, such as hormones or sweat, and release them into or onto the body.

GLUCOSE A type of sugar that circulates in the blood and provides cells with their major source of energy.

HOMEOSTASIS The maintenance of stable conditions, such as temperature or amount of water or glucose, inside the body so that cells can work normally.

HORMONE A chemical messenger that is made by an endocrine gland and carried in the blood to its target tissue or organ.

IMMUNE SYSTEM A collection of cells in the circulatory and lymphatic systems that track and destroy pathogens (germs) to protect the body from disease.

KERATIN The tough, waterproof protein found inside the cells that make up the hair, nails, and upper epidermis of the skin.

LYMPH The fluid that flows through the lymphatic system from tissues to the blood.

MEMBRANE A thin layer of tissue that covers or lines an external or internal body surface. Also the outer layer of a cell.

MENINGES The protective membranes that cover the brain and spinal cord.

MENSTRUAL CYCLE The sequence of body changes, repeated roughly every 28 days, that prepare a woman's reproductive system to receive a fertilized egg.

METABOLISM The chemical processes that take place in every cell in the body, resulting, for example, in the release of energy and growth.

MIDWIFE A specialized nurse who is trained to assist women before giving birth and during the delivery of their babies.

MOLECULE A tiny particle that is made up of two or more linked atoms.

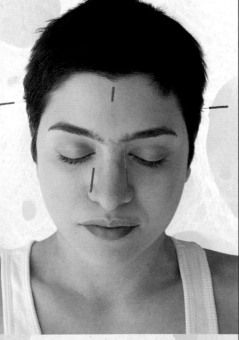

Acupuncture needles inserted into the skin to provide pain relief

Neurons in the body's communication network

NEURON One of the billions of linked nerve cells that carry electrical signals and make up the nervous system.

NUTRIENT A substance, such as glucose (sugar), needed in the diet to maintain normal body functioning and good health.

OLFACTORY To do with the sense of smell.

ORGAN A body part, such as the brain or heart, that is made up of two or more types of tissue and carries out a particular function.

OSSIFICATION The process of bone formation when cartilage is replaced by bone tissue.

OVUM A female sex cell, also called an egg.

PATHOGEN Also called a germ, a type of microorganism, such as a bacterium or virus, that causes disease in humans.

PHYSICIAN A doctor qualified to practice medicine or the diagnosis, treatment, and prevention of disease.

PHYSIOLOGY The study of the body's functions and processes—how the body works.

PLACENTA The organ that delivers food and oxygen to a fetus from its mother. Half of the placenta develops from the mother's body, the other half is part of the fetus's body.

PREGNANCY The period of time between an embryo implanting in the uterus and a baby being born, usually 38–40 weeks.

PUBERTY The period of time, during adolescence, when a child's body changes into that of an adult and the reproductive system starts to work.

SEM (SCANNING ELECTRON MICROGRAPH) An image of a specimen viewed with a scanning electron microscope.

SPERM Male sex cells, also called spermatozoa.

SPINAL CORD A column of nervous tissue that runs down the back, within the bones of the spine. It relays nerve signals between the brain and body.

Sutures, or jigsawlike joints in the skull

SURGERY The treatment of disease or injury by direct intervention, often using surgical instruments to open the body.

SUTURE An immovable joint such as that between two skull bones.

SYNAPSE A junction between two neurons, where a nerve signal is passed from cell to cell. The neurons are very close at a synapse, but they do not touch.

SYSTEM A collection of linked organs that work together to perform a specific task or tasks. An example is the digestive system.

TEM (TRANSMISSION ELECTRON MICROGRAPH) An image of a specimen viewed with a transmission electron microscope.

THORAX The upper part of the torso, also known as the chest, which is between the neck and abdomen.

TISSUE An organized group of one type of cell, or similar types of cells, that works together to perform a particular function.

TORSO The central part of the body, also known as the trunk, made up of the thorax and abdomen.

TOXIN A poisonous substance. Toxins may be released by disease-causing bacteria.

UMBILICAL CORD The ropelike structure that connects a fetus to the placenta.

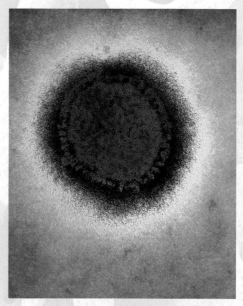

TEM of an influenza (flu) virus magnified 135,000 times

URINE A liquid produced by the kidneys that contains wastes, surplus water, and salts removed from the blood.

VEIN A blood vessel that carries blood from the body tissues toward the heart.

VIRUS A nonliving pathogen that causes diseases, such as colds and measles, in humans.

X-RAY A form of radiation that reveals bones when projected through the body onto film.

Index

Acknowledgments

Dorling Kindersley would like to thank:
Rajeev Doshi at Medimation (pp. 26–27, 28–29, 40–41, and 50–51) & Arran Lewis (pp. 38–39) for illustrations; Hilary Bird for the index; David Ekholm-JAlbum, Sunita Gahir, Andrea Mills, Susan St. Louis, Lisa Stock, & Bulent Yusuf for the clip art; Sue Nicholson & Edward Kinsey for the wall chart; Monica Byles for proofreading; Margaret Parrish & John Searcy for Americanization.

The publisher would like to thank the following for their kind permission to reproduce their photographs:

(Key: a-above; b-below/bottom; c-center; f-far; l-left; r-right; t-top)

akg-images: 9cl, 11tl; **Alamy Images:** Mary Evans Picture Library 9tl, 9tr, 10cl, 12c, 12tl, 18cla, 30cra, 33tr, 34bc, 36tl, 47cl, 56tr; Dennis Hallinan 66bc; INTERPHOTO Pressebildagentur 42br; The London Art Archive 55tr; PHOTOTAKE Inc. 7c, 26bl, 29cra, 60c; The Print Collector 12cb, 16tl, 44cr, 50tr, 56crb, 60cr; Michael Ventura 15tr; World History Archive 29tl; **The Art Archive:** Bodleian Library, Oxford / Ashmole 399 folio 34r, 10tl; Private Collection / Marc Charmet 14tr; **The Bridgeman Art Library:** Bibliothèque de la Faculté de Médecine, Paris / Archives Charmet 46cl; Bibliothèque Nationale, Paris 8cr; Private Collection / Photo Christie's Images 63br; **Corbis:** Bettmann 24tl, 26cl, 41c, 50cl, 67bc; Christophe Boisvieux 31crb; CDC/ PHIL 13tr; EPA / Geoff Caddick 69bl; Frank Lane Picture Agency / Ron Boardman 13crb; The Gallery Collection 31tl, 44clb; Hulton-Deutsch Collection 22tr, 27ca, 49bl; Gianni Dagli Orti 32c; Reuters / David Gray 69c; Ariel Skelley 62tr; Visuals Unlimited 7cr, 18clb, 19tr; Zefa / Flynn Larsen 33br; **DK Images:** The British Museum, London 42tl; The British Museum, London / Peter Hayman 8–9b, 66cl; Combustion 46–47c, 71bl; Courtesy of Denoyer – Geppert Intl / Geoff Brightling 55bc; Donks Models / Geoff Dann 13c; Arran Lewis 38–39; Linden Artists 57br; Medi-Mation 40–41c, 50–51bc; Courtesy of the Museum of Natural History of the University of Florence, Zoology section 'La Specola' / Liberto Perugi 11cr, 37tc, 44tr; Old Operating Theatre Museum, London / Steve Gorton 2cb, 4tr, 10–11b, 11cl; Courtesy of The Science Museum, London/ Adrian Whicher 8cl; Courtesy of The Science Museum, London / Dave King 3tl, 12cl, 12cr, 66cr, 69cr; Courtesy of The Science Museum, London / John Lepine 67tl; Jules Selmes and Debi Treloar 35tc; **Getty Images:** AFP / Andre Durand 15br; AFP / Damien Meyer 21br; Henry Guttmann 11tr; Hulton Archive 35br; The Image Bank / Johannes Kroemer 70bl; Nick Laham 53tr; Win McNamee 65tl; Michael Ochs Archives 48cb; Popperfoto 28clb; Science Faction / David Scharf 33cr; Science Faction / Rawlins – CMSP 64crb; Stone / Ron Boardman 13bc; Taxi / Emmanuel Faure 15bl; Time Life Pictures / Mansell 37br; Topical Press Agency 41cr; Visuals Unlimited / Michael Gabridge 71bl; **Gunther von Hagens' BODY WORLDS, Institute for Plastination, Heidelberg, Germany, www.bodyworlds.com:** 68b; **Courtesy of The Health Museum, Houston:** 69tl; **iStockphoto.com:** 8tl; Roberto A. Sanchez 16bl; Jaroslaw Wojcik 64bc; **The Kobal Collection:** Carolco 65bl; Gaumont 46tl; Warner Bros 63tr; **Library Of Congress, Washington, D.C.:** Cornish & Baker 63cr; **Mary Evans Picture Library:** 40bl; **Courtesy of The Old Operating Theatre, Museum & Herb Garret, London:** 68tr; **PA Photos:** AP Photo / Brian Walker 65tr; **Photolibrary:** Imagestate / David South 65bc; **Photo Scala, Florence:** The Museum of Modern Art, New York 31cra; **Science Photo Library:** 14cl, 23c, 25tr, 36cla, 59tl; Juergen Berger 64tr; Biology Media 25ca; Dr Goran Bredberg 37cr; A. Barrington Brown 62cla; Scott Camazine, Sue Trainor 18tl; Chemical Design 47cr; CNRI 38bl, 41bc, 49cl, 49fcl; Christian Darkin 65crb; Equinox Graphics 70cb; Eye of Science 55tl; Simon Fraser 15c; GCa 17br; Steve Gschmeissner 19br, 32tr, 51tl; Innerspace Imaging 50bl; ISM / Alain Pol 57cr; Christian Jegou Publiphoto Diffusion 6tl; Nancy Kedersha 30br; James King-Holmes 67cr; Patrick Landmann 64cl; Dr Najeeb Layyous 61tl; Astrid & Hanns-Frieder Michler 41cl; Prof. P. Motta / Dept. of Anatomy / University 'La Sapienza', Rome 39br; 54cl; MPI Biochemistry/ Volker Steger 65c; Dr Gopal Murti 62clb; NIBSC 71cr; Susumu Nishinaga 64–65 (Background), 66–67 (Background), 68–69 (Background), 70–71 (Background); Omikron 35cb; US National Library of Medicine 28tr; Wellcome Department of Cognitive Neurology 15cl; Zephyr 14bc; **Still Pictures:** The Medical File / Charles Brooks 15tl; Ed Reschke 21cb; **Wellcome Library, London:** 6bl, 16cla, 22tl, 23bc, 23tc, 36cb, 38tc, 42tr.

© 2008, by SOMSO models, www.somso.com: 2tr, 3tr, 4cla, 4cra, 18cr, 19ca, 24c, 27br, 30bl, 31bc, 32br, 46bl, 53bc, 53bl, 56bl, 56br, 58br, 59br, 60b, 61bl.

Wall chart: DK Images: Denoyer - Geppert Intl. br (inner ear); **Science Photo Library:** ftr (cell division).

Jacket images: *Front:* **Getty Images:** 3D4medical.com b; David Madison: tl. *Back:* **DK Images:** © 2008, by SOMSO models, www.somso.com c; **Science Photo Library:** Susumu Nishinaga tr

All other images © Dorling Kindersley
For further information see: www.dkimages.com

SOMSO MODELLE SINCE 1876